MW00472703

Heart Mind Belly
Points on the Map
of Self Discovery

Dear Amy.

Carolyn J Valenzuela

Heart Mind Belly, Points on the Map of Self Discovery

Published by Sojourn Publishing, LLC

Copyright ©2018 Carolyn J Valenzuela

Cover Design by the Author

ISBN: 978-1-62747-240-1
eBook ISBN: 978-1-62747-229-6

DEDICATION

Forlorn hearts,
misguided minds,
and hungry bellies,
breathe into pause

CONTENTS

SET THE STAGE

"An unexamined life is not worth living."

– Socrates, Greek Philosopher

S ocrates' student Plato tells the Allegory of the Cave. In the story, people knew of no other life than being chained in a cave, forced to view nothing but a single wall. That is all they knew. That is all they ever knew. All they could see was the wall.

Behind them was a fire. Between the fire and the prisoners', their captors moved forms to cast shadows on the wall. Voices echoed incoherently through the cave. There were no connections between the shadows and the voices. This was the prisoners' reality, random voices and obscure shadows cast on the wall of a cave.

If one of the prisoners was temporarily freed from their chains, to look at the fire blinded them. If they were forced to leave the cave, the sun would be too bright to bare. The newly freed prisoner experienced the fear of the unknown and confusion about what was real. That is until their eyes became accustomed to the light. Even then, the prisoner may cling to their reality of the shadows in the cave and doubt what they saw in the light.

If the prisoner returned to the cave, would they speak of the light and the forms that were not shadows? Would the prisoner share their stories? Was the prisoner relieved to return to their chains? What of us? What is more real; the shadows or the light?

The world is an amalgamation of belief systems and cultural attitudes. The truth is that everyone has a heart, a mind, and a belly. What is true is that when life becomes routine, complacency turns on the auto-pilot. We forget who we are and what we know. This book is an invitation to awaken the dulled senses and examine life through the three centers of the heart, mind, and belly.

Stories offer a way to navigate and interpret signs, symbols, and become reacquainted with curiosity to learn what is important today. Take a moment to clear the foggy filters through which life is viewed to calm the chaos of disconnected thinking, feelings, and emotions.

Time to clear the heart, mind, and belly centers of old, toxic stories that keeps one paralyzed. Ask each of the three centers to reveal how it looks to live a life of choice. Strive to move away from living with restrictions to a whole state of being present. Each of the three centers offers a way of being. Once aware of how life is from each of the three centers, the past is no longer an excuse for today. Courageously take a brave step into a balanced and harmonious life.

Humans are good. Humans analyze, appraise, and walk the path of this life with a sense of purpose. There are those whose purpose is clear and concise. While others wonder and wander.

The family unit is a cultural human safety net. Culture forms about religious beliefs and socioeconomic ideals. The unfolding life is not about what happens, but how the collective unit responds. The walk of life is about interactions with people. World events affect everyone, and world views draw people together or tears them apart. When the lights go out at night, everyone is alone on their own personal path. As the body rests, darkness summons the mind to mull and make sense of the world.

The story of life is the road of choice. Roads widen and diminish as the exploration of purpose progresses. The quest is the experience of inquiry, investigation, and revision. Different methods and patterns reveal themselves as the search of the most appealing one remains an arm's length away. The reward of the search is comfort in knowing that the world is filled with little pieces of peace in cracks and crevices.

This book's intention is a guide and encouragement for those seekers for whom life feels stagnant when not engaged. Those who seek feel the most alive when sampling new flavors of thought, courageously passing across new grounds, and intuitively navigating uncharted waters. They dare to travel in a variety of altitudes and attitudes to feel and see what others experience and perceive. To live in the fullness of potential rather than sporadically healing only the symptoms of the wounds of the limited moment. To live life is to develop a unique way to encounter a variety of cultures.

How one chooses to entertain life originates from their idea about the story of creation. Each culture has a story of how they came to be. My familiar story of creation comes from the Old Testament. There is the six days of creation and the rest of the story is about the nature of man. Other cultures take more time appreciating nature and natural order. Comparing creation stories, reveal similarities and the diversity among cultures. This holds true with comparative religions, philosophies, societies, and individuals.

Yes, this book hints of religion and philosophy. Not just one, but many. There are suggestions of thought processes, belief systems and exercise methods. This book is not a step-by-step, how-to-survive this world, carved in stone, set of instructions, but to spark a desire to uncover the best answers for internal issues. Consider all the human bodies and organisms required to exist in this world. What is true? What tools are in the toolbox of life are available? What can be called upon that offers hope? There is a choice to stay the same or step into the opportunity to explore. Become a magnet to attract information to make decisions in new, exciting ways. Break open a stale conflict with a fresh observation that allows time to rest in the goodness of life.

At the human core is the working interaction of three centers; the heart, the mind, and the belly. The three centers operate at odds or in balance. The challenge is to balance the three centers with the aim to create a respectful cooperation. When one of the centers is dominate, the other two centers suffer. This book is an exploration of possibility to learn what it means to function within a balanced, three center model.

This is different than relying wholly upon the heart, living solely in the head, or completely paralyzed by stuffing the belly with unresolved thoughts and emotions. Let's make it a habit to dive deeper than just scratching the surface and venture beyond the visible. Rather than oiling the squeaky wheel or attending to the demands of a crying child, speculate why that has come to be.

Any annoyance distracts thinking and awareness. When out of balance, by its nature, disruption demands immediate attention. Go beyond the obvious annoyance to the origin of the turmoil to address primary issues. Don't accept symptoms when the true cause remains intact. This book encourages uncovering the root of the problem to not pass this way again. Be done with it so that the next thing has an opportunity to arise. Elicit the courage to persist exposing the treasure.

The heart is the center stage from where one presents themselves to the world by unwrapping the gifts from their treasure chest. Consider the references when speaking from or about the heart. Such sayings refer to having heart, coming from the heart, or wearing the heart on one's sleeve, as well as losing the battle yet doing so with a lot of heart.

Now, the mind is always working. The mind shows up through one's attitude by presenting itself as hopeful or adverse. The hopeful way is to gather information to make up-to-date decisions based on some method of reasoning. The adverse way is to remain stuck in a rut, ruminating, and churning the same old stinking thinking.

The belly is the home of action. The belly is where the products of the heart and castles of the mind manifest in the world. If not cultivated, the heart and mind lose contact with the soft voice and end listening to the belly. When gut reactions are silenced, the body's vulnerability to craving increases. The nature of a craving is to be insatiable.

When actions come only from the heart, the heart breaks. When actions come only from the mind, the head hurts. When the belly is ignored, the belly aches. Ask the heart, mind, and belly to behave with intention. Once this is accomplished, the way to being contented reveals itself.

Being whole and complete allows life to show up. Realistic and healthy reflection has a way of revealing those things that no longer offer a benefit. The results uncover a gap between ourselves and other opinions, actions, and needs. In that space, notice what takes precedence over the mind's activity. Doing the work on ourselves offers a direct benefit. Not always immediate, but eventually, we learn to take care of and balance life, then create a model for others.

This book is about self-discovery. Be it a nugget or a new way to look at an old problem; the quest is to come into a different way of thinking. And maybe, this journey of self-discovery comes as something new. To awaken the three centers of the heart, mind, and belly, takes a little time to become more sensitive, and a lot more genuine, authentic, and present. Be bold. Break the chain that binds and let the light shine.

YOU ARE HERE

"No matter where you go, there you are."

– *Buckaroo Banzai, Space Hero*

E ach human enters this world innocent. The innocence never leaves but is forgotten through life and its lessons. Humans are both nurtured and natured by being socialized and institutionalized. The learning curve is steep, and the pace is quick. Preschool, grade school, middle school, high school, college, university, grad school and on. In between the breaks are chores and part-time jobs. There are special interests and time-consuming hobbies, crafts, trades, and careers. And then consumerism.

Money is an addiction. A little money earned, springs a desire to make more. The acquisition of money is a contributing factor to reaching goals. The choice is whether to take the journey alone or gather a tribe. The way of a tribe may include a spouse, a house, a mortgage, babies, children, and on to the expanded family. There are in-laws, out-laws and bylaws. As life goes, so does learning and gathering. Problems accompany the accumulation of money and possibly debt with other people's problems. Income fluctuates as companies close or corporations fail. Relationships suffer from lack of attention. However, none of this stops the sun from rising and setting. Days become weeks, weeks become months and months become years.

Time does not pass without a suggestion of hope for a benefit and reward.

Innocence is a birth right. When attacked or frightened, innocence burrows deep in the innermost self. Innocence looks for an opportunity to appear again. Innocence peers from behind the thick curtain of its hiding place. Innocence brushes the edge of daily life. Yet, innocence cautions against the risk of a full reveal. This human experience is a lifetime existence of trials and tribulations. The lessons gathered from all decisions fall into categories of being either gentle or rough, memories or nightmares. Each sunrise comes with an option to get up, dust off, and step forward. The key is to keep walking.

The lull of predictable events rocks the heart, mind, and belly to sleep. Shake the predictable with moments of reflection, to safely try on new beliefs, or hear how the voice sounds speaking new opinions. Alter the routine by attending a new church or joining a fitness center, adopt a new philosophy or enroll in a continuing education class; anything to start a new habit or spark an idea of how-to break an old habit. Hold the belief in the ability to do this alone or decide to ask for reassurance from a friend, counselor or sage.

Self-discovery is an adventurous quest for significance. The challenges of the quest smooth the rough edges that snag the ability to glide through life until complications slow the flow and turn sideways. The aim to be pleasing to self in balance with others, can flip to be completely absorbed in meeting the needs of others. When the cost exceeds the benefit, the call to wake up sounds.

There is a choice in the matter, there is always a choice. Either continue doing what has always been done and get the same results or choose to take a chance and alter the outcome. Choice implies that an effort is underway to attempt to find a deeper meaning in life.

One way to bring meaning into life is to organize like things in groups and assign value as to whether to keep or let go. This begins the personal examination of the things in life to get an idea of what is happening. What are the "things" in life? Things like living conditions, transportation, hobbies, employment, and clothes. Also consider the people. People who are close, such as a spouse, children, and parents. People who are important such as teachers, bosses, co-workers, and in our social network. Then there are the everyday people in the neighborhood, the things to see, the places to visit, and the stores to shop, such as the cashier at the deli and the attendant at the laundry.

Keep the grading scale simple with ones and zeros or pluses and minuses. Assign a value to each item on the list as to whether the item adds to well-being or takes away from the quality of life. Putting pencil to paper shows how life adds up.

Avoid self-criticism by refining the way the world is viewed. Have the same compassion for self as for another, that is with kindness, tolerance and loving acceptance. If this is uncomfortable, then apply the test of time. Ask whether the way things are today as worthy of remembrance by others tomorrow. What will others say during the funeral? What will they remember? What was the greatest impact? The long-term feelings and the lasting influence of behavior is what upholds the memory on those left behind. The power of interactions isn't immediately realized, but the effects echo in unpredictable ways. Years down the road, the person touched recognizes and appreciates the significance of the action. The best gift is delivered free of obligation and measured by its value from the many ways it continues to give.

Knowing oneself is one of the most important investments of time and effort. We can't know every detail of any other person, except ourselves. When we don't know, we guess. In the not knowing, greatness is silenced, and logic is skewed. The dark parts of being human feeds on doubt and hides in the shadows. More important, the essence of self becomes fractured. The intent is do no harm, but harm happens when parts of the identity are hidden from sight.

Being Human

*"The essence of being human is that
one does not seek perfection."*

– *George Orwell,*
Author and Journalist

The human condition is a compilation of bodies and systems. Each part has its own definition and function. Some human systems have physical attributes, while others are energetic. The highest level of energy or vibration of a thing is its etheric importance. The etheric is a vital energetic field in immediate contact with the physical body. The etheric connects the physical body with its other bodies and systems.

Here are five ways to understand ourselves as being human:

- The human as a set of systems. The skeletal, muscular, nervous, endocrine, cardiovascular, lymphatic, respiratory, digestive, urinary and reproductive systems.
- The Naturopathic human body. The mechanical body is a frame with working parts. Within the frame are biochemical substances and vital processes. The third part is the psychological capability of mental and emotional response.
- Ayurvedic medicine sees being human as a microcosm of a macrocosm or a cell within a universe. The body heals through its breath, the spirit of light, love, harmony, and wholeness.
- Four levels of life force energy animate the human. Life force energy or universal energy has many names. Those names include chi, Prana, vitality, aura, magnetism, or spirit.

The first and most dense level of energy is the physical body consisting of molecules and atoms.

The physical body relates to life in the literal realm. There is no hidden meaning. Things are as they seem. A table is a table.

The second level of energy is the realm of mind. The language of the mind relates through a symbolic representation of a word. The word "table" spoken, elicits a memory of "table." Everyone remembers an experience of table.

The third level of energy comes from the soul. The language of the soul is the image that comes from the stories heard about tables. Imagine King Arthur's Round Table or Jesus' table at the Last Supper. The stories or myths speak to the soul. This is the vibration invoked through the arts.

The fourth energetic level of human is Spirit. The Spirit's life force energy is all-encompassing, pure, and with intention.

- Meridians and chakras. Life force energy enters, leaves, and flows through systems of channels and whirlpools. A meridian is a route within the body which life force energy flows. Acupuncture follows a map of twelve different paths. Each path is associated with a specific organ. Points are triggered to release any blockage and maintain the flow of energy. A chakra is an Indian concept of a vortex of energy feeding the body in at least seven places of the human form. The common location for the chakras are at the top of the crown, brow, throat, heart, solar plexus, sacral and root. The crown connects with a divine source. The root grounds to the earth. In both systems, maintaining a smooth, unobstructed flow is critical to well-being.

This is a sampling of how to relate to and understand the bodies. The study of each system is limitless. The relationships between the bodies are complex. Much gratitude to the great minds that came before us. The scheme of bodies and energy for this book is simple. The focus is on the three centers of heart, mind, and belly within a shell.

The model for this shell is best represented as nesting four energetic bodies. Visualize four concentric shells with the center ball representing the dense, physical body. Moving outward, the emotional body is less dense and surrounds the physical body. The mental body encompasses the emotional body. The etheric body holds together the mental, emotional and physical bodies. The etheric body is the lightest body of all. "Ether" is a concept as ancient as the early philosophers. Plato spoke of ether as the place where the gods live. Aristotle considered ether as the fifth element. The other four elements are the terrestrial elements of earth, air, fire and water. Consider the etheric body as the realm of pure energy.

The Three Centers

"At the center of your being you have the answer;
you know who you are, and you know what you want."

– *Lao Tzu, Philosopher and Writer,*
Founder of Taoism

Many forms and systems exist to explain the inner and outer workings of being human. The heart, mind, and belly are necessary to be human. Everyone has a heart, mind, and belly. The three centers form the core from which joy and distress stem. When the world is chaotic and overwhelming, the initial reaction is to make sense of life. Aim to calm the impact of external stimulus to ease the internal struggle of heart, mind, and belly. Balance is when thoughts align with action free of judgment – with a sprinkle of love.

Life reflects how well the three centers function. When the centers function well, the energy enriches the six basic senses of sight, sound, touch, smell, taste and intelligence. Each center operates independent of the others. But, when the centers work together, a feeling of balance and well-being envelops us and the filters by which the world is viewed, are clear. All the worldly debris and discontentment bows to all that is right in the world.

The location of the heart center is the same as the heart organ and affirmed when asked to place a hand over the heart. The heart organ is tangible and holds space. The heart functions in the body as a pump to circulate blood.

Yet, the heart energy is not contained within the organ or even the physical body.

The head is a mainframe for the body's central processing unit. The head is the grand central station. This is the place that receives messages and dispatches the orders that keep the body going. When there is a disruption in the flow, confusion arises and bogs down the system. At first glance, the occurrence resembles a headache. Yet, there is nothing more than an internal pressure of trying to figure out what failed. The energy associated with the head is not the function of the brain. The energy has an intelligence of insight, intuition, and perception. Perception encourages poking at the obvious to imagine what may happen next. The energy of the head within the model of the four energy bodies is an energy allied with the mind.

The belly manages digestion, the action of transforming one thing into another. The belly processes food, feelings and thoughts to produce energy. This is the energy that fuels action. Left unattended, the belly develops a habit to automatically react rather than respond.

The centers of the heart, mind, and belly are gathering holes filled with memories and experiences of the past, present and future. Step beyond the limitation of this or that where one either lives in balance with the centers or focuses on the world. Life is limitless when embracing both the interaction between the people of the world and the internal workings of the three centers.

Life seems pleasant when the three centers appreciate the world as friendly. The three centers assess the surrounding, constant stimulus, as well as actions and reactions. So why not work to get these centers fine-tuned and healthy? Why not be the best one can be? Why not want more happiness and contentment in life?

When happiness and contentment is lacking, the void fills with real and imagined struggle. Either focus on the struggle or strive to excel, enhance, and exceed. The first sign of discomfort feels uneasy, as a call for attention or a sense of wonder about what's going on. Internalized tension creates a sense of pressure gathering in one or more of the centers. Is the heart heavy, is thinking convoluted, is the stomach upset? Disruptions tend to remain present when left unexamined. Turmoil breeds contempt when dumped in the darkness. As long as the belief that the solution exists out in the world, the upset simmers quietly.

Remove the upset from the fire that keeps it alive with a practice of introspection and reflection. Diligence uncovers opportunities to resolve being upset. Sometimes a solution comes about as a fluke or a lucky guess and a worry released lightens the load. Always, taking a simple, first step starts the journey. Forget about holding false assumptions about the journey and seek personal permission to explore a plethora of actions and random order to try a variety of possibilities to unlock and open the door to a new beginning. The execution of any good plan considers a margin for error and hope that all efforts return a reasonable sense of normal grounded in goodness. Affirm that all attempts are parts and pieces of being human on this earth, right now.

Core Essence

*"Love is the only way to grasp another human being
in the innermost core of his personality.
No one can become fully aware of the very essence
of another human being unless he loves him. By his love
he is enabled to see the essential traits and features.*

– Viktor Frankl, Neurologist and Psychiatrist

To own personal power means something different than to appear powerful. When owning power, the thoughts, words and deeds of others have less of an effect on well-being. Consider the consequences of encountering a minor automobile accident on a daily commute. The encounter disrupts the flow of traffic and impacts everyone's schedule. The role played in the accident is neither culprit nor victim. The only penalty experienced is a shift in the residual effect of being delayed. The responsible thing to do is to choose how to act during and because of the wait, whether with patience or agitation.

An accident is a circumstantial event. When dealing with people, there are levels of engagement, such as a casual acquaintance which needs less attention and maintenance than a long-term relationship. Close relationships have a predesigned reason for closeness, be it as family or friend.

The strength of the relationship depends on a high level of stickiness and confidence with a common significance to each other. To avoid stagnation, keep remembering the reason for the original attraction.

Wisdom is a living knowledge nourishing a mindset of inquiry and applied skill. Wisdom filters the essential from the conditional. Be it significant or trivial, the sleeping potential of best results lies in wait. Wisdom owns the consequences of thoughts, feelings and actions. The wisdom of the heart sweetly filters feelings from decisions. The wisdom of the mind filters with an intent to build personal history. The wisdom of the belly filters to choose direction and action. The three centers shape a system to serve as a moral foundation for how-to relate with and in the world.

Pause in those times when the experience suggests adversity. The energy of adversity speeds things up to close the gap between action and reaction. The more time spent in the gap allows a greater opportunity to choose a more appropriate response. Weigh the perceived consequence of an immediate, thoughtless reaction. Notice from which center, the heart, mind, or belly, the response originates. Being alert to the sensation, encourages the associated center to reveal itself. Notice if the reaction feels like a tickle, tightness, or pressure. Notice if the sensation feels hot or cold. There may be noise or silence. There may be a sensation of color or black and white. There may be an odor or the presence of a form.

When concerned, I look for a sensation within my body. At first it feels like a tickle, a flutter. With time and persistence, the sensation manifested into something workable. The centers kindly awakened one at a time. When ready, I discovered that my heart contained a piece of coal. Years later, my mind revealed the resting place of a gentle giant. Then only months after that, my belly presented itself holding a lump of clay.

These three items, the coal, gentle giant, and lump of clay, are as different as can be. Each item, each center, needed its own unique attention. Each center requires a different set of tools to work through to an agreement. The work is an investment of time, to reflect, and to craft a heart-felt commitment to map self-discovery to get through to the other side of the story.

On the other side of the story, is a whisper of who we are and what we want from life. Once the nature of each of the three centers is poked, the work continues. The three centers learn the dance of life. The dance is a simple way to be aware of the rhythm of habitual thought and thoughtless actions. The activity to get to know yourself asks only for a little quiet and a sense of wonder. The language of the mind is an exercise to play with symbols. To receive a symbol from one of the centers is a starting place. A sense of play offers a comfortable space to explore and to wonder how a symbol shows up in life as an invitation to examine different ways of being.

The heart, mind, and belly centers offer a unique essence, that when bound together, form the core. The core is designed to contain an essential blend of energies from the three centers. Essence is the blend of qualities that are true for each of us. Essence is not in the label assigned as a teacher, a doctor or an engineer. The root of self comes about through the results of "being" those things. Essence is not doing the role of mother, but the energy comes about because of "being" mother. The essence of the core is the energetic way of accepting how we came to be in this world.

The acceptance is magic. The significance of the core's essence, comes from the act of molding the energy into a form. The form complements the resilience of intention. When life is unkind, defense mechanisms activate and triggers the attempt to hide the truth and subdue one's natural essence. Then comes an effort to calm or silence the essence when it does not serve the situation. Those are the times to wake up, power up, defend and protect, in any way possible.

One center may dominant more than the other two. One center may be less mature or remains broken. Beckoned to be great or not, the three centers blend to create its essence of being. The blend, the essence, functions well or not. One's essence may be to push buttons and pull strings like a battered mess, as another is to create peace.

Essence is what makes a human, human. When not challenged, actions form habits and customs. After years without interruption, the way one begins and ends the day becomes a custom. Beyond the custom lies choice. One choice is to welcome the day with a smile and end the evening with a prayer of thanksgiving. After repeated bumps and cruel words, the pattern may shift. Rather than being grateful, it may be easier to disavow the day with a dreadful curse from sunrise. One curse begets another to end the day by planting seeds of worry. There is no begging for one more chance. Every moment of the day weeps with "what ifs" and "if only." While lamenting in darkness, the light of purity fades. When stuck in darkness, everything appears murky.

Remember, we are born innocent… and life has a way of knocking the innocence right out of us. This is unfortunate. The results of filtering influence perception. Coming from a place of innocence is a factor in how the centers filter the experience of the world. Innocence perceives blamelessness. An event filtered through a perverted filter is likely to see doubt and negativity. When attacked, the center shuts down rather than participate in a senseless battle. With a little attention to the core, years of neglect melt away to renew that which is true for you.

Each of the centers operate with a different set of tools, which produce a different kind of energy. Feelings and emotions are not restricted to the heart. Thinking is not restricted to the mind. To understand the core, consider the qualities each of the three centers offer.

Consider the qualities of the heart. Emotion and feelings appear to identify as coming from the heart. Love, compassion, kindness. Peace, ease, warmth. Valentine's Day is a fine example of the array of emotions and feelings about matters of the heart. The pendulum of emotions swings from levels and kinds of love to the agony of betrayal.

The quality of the mind is separate from the function of the brain. The brain is the body's command and control center. Headaches suggest abusing the gray matter like straining a muscle while lifting weights. Does the mind ache because of exercising too many thoughts, too many times, of too much weight?

The belly is the powerhouse, an area from below the bottom rib down to the pelvic bone, front and back of the body. When the abdominals are worked, the back is strengthened. Too much focus on tightening the muscles restricts the natural action of the belly.

The belly churns, turns, and burns everything eaten. When the belly is abused, the belly retaliates. The mass of unprocessed thoughts and emotions weighs heavy on the belly. The natural state of the belly is to process all that enters and move it through. When refusing to let go, the belly continues to cycle. The belly has an intelligence. When the system bogs down, signals of distress pass to the brain. When ignored, the initial distress manifests an experience of upset, disruption, or regurgitation. A doctor can prescribe a remedy to cover up the upset and force the system to keep running, but the upset stews until a solution to uproot the seed occurs. The nature of this dynamic system is the essence of the belly.

Birth of a "Spark"

"From a tiny spark may burst a mighty flame."

– Dante, Poet and Moral Philosopher

Wakening awareness takes effort. There is no off switch to turn on awareness. The process may appear simple, but it is not easy. There is no single approach that allows one to sit down and force one's way into awareness. Awareness can't be forced to push its way to the surface. Doing so would be like straightening a water hose by pushing it. The hose ends up in a pile no further than the farthest point from the beginning of the exercise.

Awareness sparks as the result of a gentle nudge. Quiet the small voice to hear the rustlings of possibility coming from the heart, mind, or belly. Request that the noise continues until it makes sense. For a message to make sense needs vigilance. What is meaningful to one person may confuse the next. Question, wait, and confirm until the essence of the message is true for you.

Ask for the wisdom of a situation. Wisdom sparks a soft counter to a harsh judgment or uncovers a once hidden common-sense solution. Suspend reasoning, silence the inner critic, and calm the ego. Allow the still, small voice to speak. A flash of inspiration hints of hope where nothing existed. The spark bridges the gap between here and there. Surrender to the way things are with a willingness to consider a new way.

The spark is like a new pair of glasses to see fresh perspectives. The perspective was always there. Now there is a new way of seeing something as never before or failed to see in the first place. In either instance, that what was invisible is now evident.

Understanding Words Have Power

"Words: So innocent and powerless as they are, as standing in a dictionary, how potent for good and evil they become in the hands of one who knows how to combine them."

– Nathaniel Hawthorne, Novelist and Short Story Writer

According to the Oxford Dictionary: un·der·stand·ing is

1. Sympathetically aware of other people's feelings; tolerant and forgiving: "people expect their doctor to be understanding"

2. Having insight or good judgment.

To be in a place of understanding encourages healing and well-being, a state of flow rather than stagnation. Sympathy is the spirit of knowing more is happening than what is visible. Understanding is the ability to be free of judgment and the need to know every detail while patiently holding space for a situation to evolve with everyone concerned.

To understand feels right. When something doesn't feel right, chances are it isn't. When bewildered, it is because pieces of the puzzle are missing. The missing information may be withheld by choice, disregarded as unimportant, or hidden in the fringe of a story. Nothing feels right or resolved until the details are known.

The opposite of understanding is confusion. When the immediate response is more aggressive than a trivial thought, the situation has sunk into a distraction. Confusion and distraction play off each other like smoke and mirrors. There are no winners in a battle of wits as the level of distraction increases, the risk of confusion intensifies. Lacing details, dazed and confused, muddled thinking resorts to applying a label on the person or issue. A label is easily relatable and glosses over the sticky, problematic parts. Labels are thoughtlessly sustained and nourished until it accepted as the truth. The label is empowered, not the thing itself. Once established, the label remains intact, yet the confusion and distraction diminish, evolve, or vanish.

Words spark energy and the energy effects the four energetic bodies. The physical body accepts the word in its most material, literal form. The emotional body fancies the energy of the word as a figure of an illustration. The mental body resonates to the symbol the word represents. The etheric body relates to the word at its most mythological interpretation. The trouble with speaking occurs when a word's dynamic nature is restricted it to its literal form. The challenge is to slow down our hearing to experience a word's vibration through all four energetic bodies; physical, emotional, mental and etheric.

Words create consequences. Once spoken, the speaker looks for a sign of connection with the audience. Be it a nod of the head or a squint of the eyes, a response from a listener confirms an interaction was constructed. Some consequences are predictable, such as the head nod or eye squint, while other outcomes are surprising.

Claiming to be a speaker of words, is an assumption to know what is being said. It is naive to think that one definition is consistent in all situations. The words in front of one audience receives accolades, while another audience boos. A kind word soothes one, while the same word upsets someone else. A familiar word unintentionally can challenge reality. Words are greater than their definitions – words are subject to interpretation.

Once upon a time a man's word and a handshake was all that was necessary to seal a deal. The handshake symbolized peace; offering the hand showed there was no weapon. When the opposite hand started wielding a weapon, though, things changed. The hand shaken in good faith began to hold a moving target, while stabbing the victim with a knife in the other hand. Once a handshake suggested the possibility of drawing blood, the parties began to sit down with a table between them. A signature on a contract replaced the handshake. The pen became mightier than the sword. The written word was stronger than the spoken word.

Messy words, like labels, tend to invoke images associated with harsh emotions. The use of the word when referencing people, solidifies its definition. The definition bows to its lowest understanding. Such labels as poor performer, convict, slave keep people contained. Such messy words like poverty and enough keep groups of people controlled.

Poverty is the state of being poor. Impoverished is being distressed, indigent, broke, worse than usual, and hopeless. Poverty is not restricted to the physical realm. Poverty is experienced physically, spiritually and mentally. When the body is broken, and the spirit is bankrupt, self-esteem suffers. A repressed world view restricts and limits the chance for a healthy existence. The state of poverty is contagious. Affluence attempts to protect itself by building programs to put lots of space between those who are poor and those who are not. Money alone doesn't address the problem. Food temporarily fills the belly but does not satiate the hunger for better ways and better days. Removing an obstacle without destroying the root cause of poverty guarantees its imminent return. And when it does, it picks up where it left off or has grown larger because the pain of knowing life in the light creates a greater sense of desperation. Any solution must include healing the ugly attraction to the affliction of being poor.

The word enough suggests an elusive sense of almost adequate. The messiness comes about when the definition of being enough sources from the ego. The ego defines enough as a point beyond what currently is. The ego holds no tangible limit with enough. The word enough is both qualitative and quantitative. The quality of enough is part of appearance, a value applied as good or bad and right or wrong. There seems to be never enough. When measured, it is through comparison. The scale gauges everything from need to greed, between plenty and scarcity.

The transfer of ideas is a gift when the spoken notion is received in the manner offered. When the notion is different from the concept spoken, the ears close and a gap fills with an emotional charge. The emotional charge is neutral until another word plugs the gap or a memory prompts meaning. Working through the landmines of gaps and holes becomes a conversation rich with redo and replay of noise and digestion – until the magic happens.

A word is rich with an assumed intent. Combination of words attempt to convey concepts like "love," "family," or "friend." A conversation takes time and commitment, skill and patience; time to traipse through differences, a commitment to continue to conclusion, skill to navigate in various directions, and patience to remain diligent.

A good conversation brings heaven to earth as a celebration of words and ideas. When words happen to scrape a new landscape and spring forth new ideas, the experience is blissful. Words that relate with each other create a bond that grows stronger with additional connection. As the bond grows, the construct of the topic elevates. The rapid exchange of words and ideas takes on a nature of its own. There is one stipulation. It is true simply in the moment. The sensation of connection holds only during the interaction. The likelihood of remembering the nuances of the interchange is slim. The feeling remains while the words fade. The wisdom of the exchange lasts forever. The energy of conversation alters the vibration of the four energetic bodies; the physical, emotional, mental, and etheric bodies shift.

The energy of the words power and force are different. Power is a quality that directs or influences behavior. Force is a dominating energy to coerce action. Powerful words inspire, as forceful words depress. Forceful words tend to provoke an automatic reaction. Powerful words invite support. Words of force tempt resistance.

Being in power is the ability to articulate one's needs. Knowing the difference in energy between power and force helps to uncover the language familiar to the heart, mind, and belly. Words leave the lips and drift to the ears, all the while filtering through life stories. The space between the mouth and ear is the magical world of the mind. The words may be crystal clear but passing through filters gives power to the word.

To live is to celebrate the pursuit of creative expression. As noted, the energy of words as power and force, comes through its delivery. Words can also be delivered in the lines of a poem, the lyrics of a song, and scripted for play. The written word offers the potential to influence the interpretation of the past, soothe the tensions of the present, and prepare for the coming of the future. Poem, song or script, words impact the four energetic bodies in different ways. Notice which form of the word offers its greatest impact on which body, be it physical, emotional, mental or etheric. The realization of its impact expands personal knowledge, about the heart, the mind, and the belly.

Appreciate the importance of the word, the power of its influence, and its intention through tone. A word's meaning is its definition and relationship to the power of its influence. There is power in the possibility of misinterpretation. As effective as the spoken word can be, the words left unspoken are equally important.

The Hidden Side

"Energy cannot be created or destroyed,
it can only be changed from one form to another"

– Albert Einstein, Theoretical Physicist

Words vibrate with a sense of energy. The energy of a word increases through repetition. Lovers, bullies, politicians and evangelists encourage reaction with the frequent use of charged words. Words sway opinions and navigate the course of humanity. The word becomes energetically animated by association, like when adjectives and adverbs are added to nouns and verbs. The space around a word seeks clarification. This hidden activity as the energy of a word begins with content. Content is established by its definition. Using a word establishes its context. The context of a word increases liveliness when the content can be applied to a variety of settings. The power of a word's content is its ability to alter its context. And in its repetition, the word ruffles its undertones. The content, context and energy of a word includes elements of complexity from the heart, mind, and belly, and yet, the personal experience of a word resonates more with one of the three centers than the others. This is the hidden side of a word. Playing with the idea of content, context and energy, is much easier than thinking about it. Contemplate the hidden side of the word "love."

The definition of "love" suggests affection as a verb and a noun. The content of "love" is how a person relates with affection, as with an object or as an action. When the word "love" is associated with an object or action, love is circumstantial. When speaking in a loving way, the tone of voice relays as either pleasant or unpleasant. Imagine the various forms the word "love" takes within isolated circumstances. One situation may be two lovers reacquainting themselves after an extended separation. The more complex a scenario, the more interesting the underlying motive for love to hold things together. Consider an abusive relationship. Where is the love when two people quarrel over buying a book to satisfy their child's love of reading?

Objects vibrate with a sense of energy. People, places, and things animate through energy. The flow of energy is either orderly or chaotic, expansive or contracted, fast or slow. Flow is movement in the same direction restricted only by one's ability to manage it. When the energy flow is chaotic, the lesson to learn is either open to the flow or restrict access. Without innate management skills, chaos attracts chaos. There are two responses to chaos. Chaos may be the fertile ground of creation or a tornado of emotions. Chaos may be a friend or the chance to search for ways to create a flow of energy.

The effects of energy are evident and present within the hidden side of things. When the ability to maintain flow diminishes, the energy transforms into pressure. The intensity of the pressure escalates until it alters life as it is known. The nature of the source remains unknown until it is time to be known. A force contained continues as a block from being present. Unresolved duress becomes a part of who we are; it changes our outlook. The pressure persists until becoming friends with the self to discover what is missing.

Ego, the Friend

*"The experience of the self is always a
defeat for the ego."*

– Carl Jung, Founder of Analytical Psychology

Ego is the sense of self and how one sees themselves in the world. The ego's sole purpose is to protect itself. We forget we are the caretaker of the ego because the ego is so loud. We give the ego the power to protect us from danger, and in that shift of power, the ego guards us from harm. The ego believes that the less we know, the better.

The ego demands a lot of attention. Ego is a place of judgment, desire, and the home of "me and mine." The ego has unbridled access to the full repository of our history. There are piles of recollections awaiting judgment. Ego controls the unbalanced accounts of right, wrong, and indifference. Ego maintains a perceived safe place detached from others. Ego, not knowledge, divides and separates.

Where is the "I"? The essence of "I" is a label. "I" is the language of the ego. Consider the use of the word "I." Notice when the reference of self with "I" statements, such as I am, I see, I want, I desire, I suffer, gets in the way of manifesting the essence of personal truth. "I" is a strong statement that suggests a sense of personal power. When left unchecked, the ego erects a wall of protection out of blocks of fear.

The delicate, sensitive ego does not want to be deemed the source of blame. The ego is necessary; it is best not to shut it down. Assign a fair and healthy view to ego. The ego is like a soft shell around our existence. The ego on alert, wears a bull's-eye waiting for the next unfair, infraction launched at us. Some targets are huge. Others, not so big. Some egos are bold enough to step right out there, front and center to attract the aim of others. The ego can be reserved and offer a supportive internal dialogue. Beware of a dialogue with words lacking substance. The ego feeds on a poor diet of self-serving nonsense. The ego enjoys full range access into all aspects of life. The focus on a greater good diminishes as the ego demands authority over the heart, mind, and belly.

The opening for ego to enter and assume the role of commander-in-chief, ruler, and supreme being was of our own doing. When surrendering as slave to the ego, we are at its mercy. we suffer, we moan, until we lie down. No need to get up in arms and start acting the tough one. Emotions get the revolution going, but strategy and plans get the work done. The ego will not tolerate punishment. Don't deny its existence nor downplay its relevance. Approach the ego with honor and appreciation. The ego has always been there, right, wrong or indifferent. Yet, there comes a time when enough is enough. There comes a time when the essence wants to be free from the protective biases of the ego. Although the ego ensures safety, there comes a time to take life back; to summon help from the hidden parts and call upon the wisdom of disappointment. The biggest task is to reassure the ego that it is not a target for assassination. There remains an important place for the ego. A healthy ego is supportive. Guide the ego to serve in the highest way, a way that supports the purpose.

There are times when we want something other than what is happening. We wake from a sleep state and struggle to place the ego in check. An event can be a subtle change of pace that alerts us that the status quo is no longer acceptable. The way things are, no longer suit our needs. The event can be a birthday, retirement, a wedding, a funeral, or a birth. The wake-up call can be any kind of thing, but most importantly it signals the time for change. Life is about human development, maturation, from sprout to blossom to seed. The word "change" is spot on but conjures up a list of excuses to support resistance. If the word "change" is repulsive, then find another word. Find a word appropriate for the activity to address the layer of pain numbing the need for growth. The change process can be frightening, demanding, and uncomfortable, whether it is called adjust, shift, or transform.

Hold the Soul

"The philosopher's soul dwells in his head, the poet's soul is in his heart; the singer's soul lingers about his throat, but the soul of the dancer abides in all her body.

– Khalil Gibran, Artist and Poet

Where is the soul? The soul is a piece of the Divine under our care as a citizen of this planet. Some consider the soul's home in the heart. Others consider all the thoughts about the soul would be in the head. If feelings, emotions, and thoughts balance out, then the soul comes through action. The soul defined as consciousness suggests an all-pervasive energy, an energy that has no form or no location. The purpose of the soul is to evolve, grow, and mature, until it reunites with the Divine. For some, there is no separation between the soul and the Source. Evolution, growth, and maturity spark through inquiry.

Ask the soul questions when there is adequate time to sit with an array of comebacks. Once questions of this nature begin, the mind does not stop. Am I comfortable with being who I am? Question if there is a desire to look for something more. And if the questions lead away in a different direction, come back to the question. There is no turning back. There is no unforgetting what has been recalled. We will never be that same person and that is a good thing. We can choose to stop asking questions, but we can never go back, nor backwards.

Asking the right question is less important than listening for the right answer. The right answer makes its way through and feels different than any other thoughtform. The ego's purpose is safety. Imagine what the ego hears as it filters out all perceived threats. Look for answers that feel like an epiphany or deep truth. Know that all three centers, heart, mind, and belly, and the four energetic bodies, physical, emotional, mental, and etheric, are attuned to hear. Listening from the level of the soul is an act of trust in one's ability to receive messages.

Messages come in different forms. Waiting to hear the words, may miss the symbol. Waiting to catch a symbol, may miss the message in the song playing on the radio. Depending upon the radio may blur the pertinent storyline of a movie. Listening from the soul requires the development of a specific mind set. This listening is a sense greater than what the ears hear and the eyes see. The message may come as a feeling, a sensation, a knowing. Listen from the heart. Listen from the mind. Listen from the belly. Listen from the soul. The message may be as subtle as a shift in perception. What is true today, may not be true tomorrow and don't wait. The message is valid when it feels true.

THE HEART

"You have to keep breaking your heart until it opens."

– Rumi, Poet and Theologian

My heart center was the first to soften enough to bring to light its brokenness. I sat on the sofa in the front room of my friend, a newly certified yoga instructor, tarot card empath. I offered to help her collect her practicum hours for certification. A common prompt spoken while moving through yoga poses is to breathe into the pose and open the heart. She perceived my heart held back from opening to its fullest. She sensed a dark spot on its surface. As I defended my closed heart, I wondered what purpose was served by a life that consisted of reiterating painful life stories. Her questions followed a path paved by the tarot cards she randomly tossed on the sofa's cushion that separated us. I rolled over old stones and crawled through endless wormholes as I told my history of events and individuals whom had crossed me. One of the last times we were together, as she tossed cards, she asked about my spouse. In the space between her question and my answer she injected her observation. Of all the people I spoke of and all the events I had shared, I avoided mentioning his name. Her question poked the dark spot on my heart. The spot responded with a spark and magnified in space and density. The dark spot felt like a chunk of coal, not soft, but very, very hard. It was cold and heavy. She suggested I spend quiet time with my chunk of coal until our next meeting.

Her four-word question "what of your spouse" drilled to the center of the small, insignificant dark spot. With this ever so slight consideration, my heart tempered. I was being asked to relate my thoughts about my relationship. An innocent act, this harmless inquiry startled the hard, cold chunk of coal enough for it to begin to unwind. The numbness initiated a sense of tingling. The hardness softened to expose the presence of layers. As the form of the coal swelled, space separated the layers in such a way to thin, separate and peel back to expose the next underlying layer. Each layer embodied a disappointment hiding from acknowledgement. The thickness of the layer exemplified the intensity of recollected pain from the original transgression. Pain restricts what is seen by the eyes, neither the depth nor the origin of the memory. I was years beyond the need to understand the significance of each layer. My intent was to find what was below the layers. I wanted to know what was at the core. I wanted to step away from pain and uncover my defiant form of self-love.

Once the layers of coal evaporated, all that remained was a dirty, worn out treasure chest. The lock slipped off and the lid beckoned to be lifted to reveal its contents. Opening the treasure chest was like opening Pandora's Box. All the things I had stuffed away as too painful to hold flooded my world. My memories had not served me well. There was no magic. The memories had not transformed into neatly packaged lessons. Time erodes the details of an event, leaving raw emotions to float about craving to be forgiven. In the energy of that moment, the filth acted as a magnet for all the wrongs of the world, all the feelings of pain, negativity, and betrayal to let themselves be known. As quickly as the moment came, it passed, leaving the fear that my vulnerabilities would take control as I faced my naked self.

In a place of openness, there is nowhere to hide. All that was revealed won't fit back in its container. The tools used to get here no longer work. Confidence waivers, self-esteem suffers, and innocence is completely lost. All that remains is burden and blame.

Sweet Innocence

*"The innocent and the beautiful
have no enemy but time."*

– William Butler Yeats, Poet and Playwright

Innocence is one of the final layers of the protective embryotic sack from seed to toddler. Innocence is the sweet state of being free from guilt and blame, to hold little thought of anything other than peace in the present moment. The small child doesn't make up the sensation of lack. Lack, guilt, and blame are brought to our attention. Innocence under attack is like waiting for shades of darkness to descend, separate, and leave the fear of being alone. To engage darkness requires a courageous review of what died or went missing. Death is never the end but provokes the next opportunity for growth. Missing parts leave a gap in the heart. Chinese lore professes that the crack in a bowl repaired with gold is the strongest part of the dish. Equally true of the broken heart. The healed wound is stronger but the softness that holds the repair in place remains vulnerable.

There is no set point loss of innocence, there is the process of losing. The harm may come about as a result of an incident that shook reality, maybe something more subtle like a constant wave that undermined a sense of stability. Nonetheless, life that had once been is no more. The details of the circumstances fade, yet the instability remains. The void smells of a sense of guilt and weighs heavy in responsibility for the world. Color this with a quiet shame of not understanding why. There is no scale of balance in reaction to a situation that awakens the historic feeling. The most recent harm will awake the sleeping response as if it were the first time. The consequence is an unrelenting repetition of the same thought about the same detail. Whether innocence is surrendered or stolen, there is suffering in replaying the loss over and over again. No longer innocent, there is no longer trust that the world is safe.

Innocence in the face of the adult is not as sweet as the innocence in the face of the child. No child's face ought to bear witness to the ugliness of war, or the pangs of hunger, or the emptiness of abandonment. Innocence is a birthright, coming into this world without sin and doing no wrong. Sin is the stripping away the innocence of a child. Adults lacking innocence are deficient in a healthy self-esteem, unpolluted of ulterior motive. The strength to stand firmly on moral ground, succumbs to a lesser option of playing the role of martyr, antagonist, or facilitator. Sporting a mask may seem safer than being authentic. Virtue and inspiration melt against the feeling of lack. That sensation of not being or having enough is disguised by desire, want, or need.

The quickest return to innocence is a curious heart. Permit stale observations to germinate the seeds of questions to sprout fresh answers. The willingness to investigate and examine the present rearranges fixtures to make space for newly discovered ideas. This also requires a willingness to invest time to massage resistance to be soft and comfortable to agree to the possibility of change. These are tiny, innocent steps. When ready, the layers covering the treasure chest peel themselves back. Debris and obstacles are cleared away. Detours no longer serve a purpose. The process to discover the points on the path back to an authentic self is revealed.

The Heart Contained

"The human heart has hidden treasures,
In secret kept, in silence sealed;
The thoughts, the hopes, the dreams, the pleasures,
Whose charms were broken if revealed."

– Charlotte Bronte, Novelist and Poet

The innocent heart, like an energy vortex, like water, expands to its point of least resistance. Unlimited by potential and boundless by space, the heart naturally resilient and persistent stays buoyant. The heart doesn't keep score if there is a speck of hope or a smidgen of encouragement. The heart gauges flow as high or low rather than switch on and off. Once a cold calculation slows the stream, emotions slow down, and responses feel predictable. The answers are known before the question is asked.

The hinges of a treasure chest grow rusty and refuse to allow access to its resources. Safe guarding the chest chokes the experience of life with an unproductive purpose. Negativity, criticism, and calculation holds no space. The flow of this dark matter is dense and heavy, but not expansive. The tide continues and feeds upon itself. False pride radiances in being able to consume more darkness which offers little benefit and stagnates growth. Disrupt the flow and let the magic happen. Open the heart to the possibility of life being different.

Imagine a life so full of potential that the container that holds the heart becomes too small. Imagine existing in a place that confines the spirit. To trust that the spirit of potential exists in all other people is the same trust required to break open and spill the perpetual essence of the heart into the world. Threats and fears return again and again until faced and resolved in expressions of truth and love.

A healthy internal dialogue serves as an aide in surviving scary situations and frightening people. If the voice inside the head were just one, there would be no dialogue. Play with the idea of more than one voice because the dialogue is incessant. Voices from the heart, voices from the head and voices from the belly, all demand attention. Emotions, thoughts, and feelings have a voice and a weight. To move from unhealthy to healthy, prepare to listen to the cacophony of voices and press beyond the limits of the container.

The area that lies beyond the surface value of a thing is truly a safe place to explore its untarnished nature. There, the inquiry of resistance toward a situation or person can be done with less interruption and greater clarity. The sidelines aren't a place to learn how the game is played. Humans tend to hesitate until completely prepared. Fear of the unknown incapacitates participation. One's own or even another's experience suggests the steps of proper preparation. There is no need to perfect the ability to leap to the top of the mountain in a single bound. Strength, ability, and confidence build by taking little steps. Be willing to circle around a single issue until a greater understanding of the whole is collected. Calling upon patience to nibble away smalls bits uses less energy and gains just as much ground, if not more than taking on the whole. The gathering of personal power and courage to map the way is more peaceful and responsive than blindly pounding away with force. The face of power and courage sourced from love inspires. The heart can no longer be contained, but rather the home base for self-discovery.

Map the Heart

"All things are difficult before they are easy."

– Thomas Fuller, Churchman and Historian

Discovering one's internal compass is a gift. When living in ignorance about the care of the heart, the heart screams, "Look at me." The pain of remaining the same is greater than the fear of the risk to crack open the container. Dare to undertake the indefinite task of working through uncertainty for the chance of a better way. Penetrating the layers of protection surrounding the heart requires an honest approach and attention to detail. The journey to the heart requires a diligent, steadfast, and conscious intention. The lower, deep-rooted layers, once tapped, reveal more layers. The layers seem like they never end. Resistance gnaws at the tough and persistent ego, dedicated to protecting the heart at any cost. By design, the ego keeps the landscape of resistance a secret. Until the ego becomes an ally, the soft, vulnerable heart remains contained.

In the moment that everything seems to be wrong and nothing seems to be right, the spark of hope for a brighter tomorrow rouses. Excavation begins by breaking the ground with a simple question. Remember the first time the heart experienced being broken? The event may have been as innocent as a normal childhood event, like getting separated and lost in a store. Perhaps there was trauma during potty training or drama with the first day of school.

A natural human function may be associated with an uncomfortable embarrassment.

A change of habit when forced may cause a devastating blow to an early reality. Imagine a scenario so severe that childhood curiosity fades into darkness. The way hurt and disappointments are handled as a child, follows through into adulthood. Effective and ineffective behaviors attempt to ignore or extinguish the sting of upsets. Life is the accumulation and distribution of little inequities. Then, along comes be one big hurt that keeps resurfacing and reinjuring the wound. A child is unaware of the damage that comes about by holding on instead of dealing with the hurts.

Avoiding pain is painful in and of itself. Love left unexpressed is a love that withers and dies. Time doesn't heal all wounds. The passage of time nourishes the layers of protection against injustice, disrespect, and disregard. Good people collect a warehouse of uncomfortable memories and create a volume of names associated with hurt and transgressions. Somewhere along the line, the memories, the people, and transgressions are reduced to a single name. And that one name holds the responsibility for an entire lifetime of hurt. All triggers learn to react to that single name. All the earlier instances, the faces, the places, and all other culprits are filed away to be forgotten. That one name presents the opportunity for history to be stuffed into a single box, sealed tight, and marked done.

The name becomes the label of the container. Believe it or not, there is choice in the relationship with that name, that container. The name becomes the excuse for all the evil in our world, for all the reasons to engage or disengage, and justification for hiding. Great lengths are taken to avoid mentioning the name. Yet, saying that name could be the very key that unlocks the way to begin the journey of reconciling with the heart. Our willingness to face injury is the spark that reignites love left dormant until now. Does the ability to give love and expect nothing in return exist?

Love, when contingent on the availability of another human, is not love, but addiction. Love is conditional when reliant on someone else's happiness. Conditional love presents itself as a game of this for that, tit for tat, give and take. Love, when questioned, shines light on the recesses of a false concept about the relationship. Somewhere in the darkness the seed of conditional love fans the flame that awakens the heart. The name that had once silenced and imprisoned the heart, now releases the power to unravel the tie that binds. Liberated unexpressed emotions echo in the heart.

Any hint of ownership between two people begins to encase both hearts, both treasure chests that contain all that is good and loving in this life. When the good and loving fades, the treasure chest protects itself with thick layers of blame and denial. The layers transform the treasure chest into a tomb. Instead of living, the heart withdraws from love and retreats into its organic function as a pump and valve for blood.

The successful uncovering of the tomb requires a plan, a set of steps and reasons. Proceed with caution and a toolbox of contingencies in case the path leads to a dead end or conceals booby traps. Mapping the convoluted journey to and through the tomb acts as a journal to not pass this way again without forewarning. Become familiar with paths crossed and trails that led nowhere. Attempt to avoid repeating the same mistakes but be willing to do so until the lesson is learned. A map shows what is missing and places yet to be visited. A map exposes alternate routes for returning to love. A map liberates the prisoner and records a sometimes-disorienting release of memories. A map acts as a reminder of the migration in and out of the depressions of the heart.

Weather the Storm

*"Maybe you have to know the darkness
before you can appreciate the light."*

– Madeline L'Engle, Writer

Within a hardened heart, fear stagnates relationships. Fear disguises itself as pain, rejection, and/or abandonment, but fear is fear nonetheless. Habits are created to survive bad relationships. Habits are easier to let go of when life is comfortable and has a direction. A hole in the soul left unattended, remains where habits once resided. Choose to fill the void left by the roots of destructive habits with seeds of hope.

The journey of self-discovery may not need new sights, but rather the ability to see old ways with fresh eyes. When the tomb opens, look to see a symbol coming from the treasure chest, a symbol of hope to carry the rest of the way. The symbol may be a number, a feather, or a sound that will show up as a reminder of the journey. Simply accepting the symbol begins the process for layers of hurt to fall away. A new world filled with a set of fresh, bare vulnerabilities. Each vulnerability comes with a new form of hurt. Each step tests one's level of commitment, strength and resolve. On the path of self-discovery, challenges are temporary and make the journey more important. Remain steadfast and true to the cause by holding firm to the symbol of hope.

My symbol of hope was the idea of "gift," a beautifully presented souvenir of the unknown. Opening the treasure chest left me feeling anguish and guilt. I harbored such an ill will toward the one I loved that I was attracted and repelled at the same time. I wanted to express my love in a new way and rejected intimacy for not having been present in the relationship. The resentment toward the name resumed in a new fashion. Not wanting to return to the way I had been, the "gift" offered a new expression of hope. I was to act "as if" until it was true. My nature is to be kind and thoughtful. I wasn't being true to my nature because I was stuck in relationship with the name. I stopped making kindness and caring personal and started doing it because that is what I am. I stopped giving morning kisses to the name and started giving kisses because that is who I am. I stopped giving gifts to the name and gave gifts because that is what I do. There was my hope. There was "I" coming back to myself.

I was excited to be reacquainted with myself. This give and take, two steps forward, was a vulnerable moment. When I withdrew into my self-created tomb, everything around me suffered. I appeared lifeless. When I side-stepped the role of the victim, I stopped reacting to attacks. Attacks are pointless and no longer serve a purpose when the victim steps into being themselves. There is no reason to continue suffocating something when it is already dead. If an action intends to elicit a certain reaction, and there is no reaction, then the action is a failure. If a relationship depends on pleasure through pain, and pleasure is gone, a search for a new pain is under way.

Not all relationships make it through the process of uncovering the heart. As I followed my map, walked my journey, and held my symbol of hope, those around me placed their importance of our relationship on hold. They are left to wonder and wait, until I emerged through the crack of a soft, vulnerable underside of who I once was. Unintentional or not, my new face cried out, "Hey, look at me!" Others' reactions felt like personal attacks. Be advised, no one is comfortable with change. Do not take things personally. Know that people tend to act the same way, regardless to whom they direct their actions. The engagement always says more about them than who they direct their words and actions. Stand strong in a space to watch an attack impersonally. Yet, it still happens; the attacks still hurt.

Peeling back the protective layers of the tomb agitates underlying emotional responses. These emotions had remained hidden from all concerned. The reactions of others witnessing emotional revelations vary from eliciting support to conjuring fear. The witness comes from their own self-interest. To them, my situation was invisible, not in a mean or cruel way, just unnoticed. My suffering was silent. Their focus was in a different direction.

Trying on new ways of being is a matter of trial-and-error. Time spent practicing on how-to recognize an old way of being is fruitless. The return of an old way is not blatant nor easily recognizable. With little fanfare, unexamined ways of being gently seduce a vulnerable soul's revisit to inattentive behavior. A longstanding offense and deeply imbedded habits rarely return in the same manner under the same circumstance.

The beauty in owning the question that seeded the winds of change and stoked the fire storm of emotions, is opening the treasure chest to be wrapped in a blanket of love rather than denial because of a name. The name is only the symbol of a struggle. Life is a struggle to break free from being chained to the past and become comfortable when releasing the security of being anchored to outdated thinking. Something happens to kick us from the safe nest and learn to fly, something always happens. How deep is the attachment to the life-altering experience? The intent of learning is not to organize the details of every infraction of life. There is no wisdom in the details nor any benefit to replay broken records. Broken records get stuck in the same place. Growth is not in the hashing out what went wrong with each person and every event. Search for a heart within the story of life as a dream. Uncover the delicate heart to come into light and shine in the fullness of self.

Love Energy Light

"Don't cry because it's over, smile because it happened."

– Dr. Seuss, Writer and Illustrator

The power of love comes through as energy and light. The strength of love is its vitality beaming through every living entity. We reflect the love in our lives. Life thrives through being engaged and moved by interaction. Layers of darkness that once concealed the treasure chest within the heart have been invited to fall away.

The energy of love springs from the heart center to clear the course. The once stagnant energy rekindles the likeness of flow. Detour signs vanish leaving the way open for all that is new. Filters are wiped clean of memories no longer controlling the emotions. Fresh eyes gaze upon what had been invisible.

Eyes that no longer see the light of love remain in darkness. Ask the heart to give permission to turn on the light and view the world in a whole new way. Unencumber the light from the shades of the past and the soiled filters once used to view the world. Let the light shine through limited perceptions of right and wrong. Let the light be independent and optimistic about the future. In this moment, be free from old stories and unrealistic expectations.

Love is naturally unconditional and free of expectation. Unconditional love does not expect a measured exchange. Unconditional love is any act done free from hope of return. The gift of love is pure from the expectation of recognition. Develop the process of calling on patience to permit the yearning for acknowledgement of an act to soften into love. The passage of time quickens its pace with each opportunity to accept that the act is a state of love unto itself. Be able to spread love and avoid getting caught in the act.

Sharing the love, distributing the energy, and diffusing the light hold like benefits of paying kindness forward. An altruistic nature still serves the self with a feeling of being a part of something good. Spreading goodness softens hard edges and cushions other's rough experiences. A hand extended to lift another is a welcomed relief.

Love, energy, and light are neither quantified nor restrained in its current container. Once the map of the heart has been laid out and followed to its full expression, directions are no longer needed. The heart is bigger than its container. The heart is no longer closed and the treasure chest overflows with gifts that keep giving.

Fair Warning

*"We are like chameleons, we take our hue and the color
of our moral character, from those who are around us."*

– John Locke, Philosopher and Physician

To be present in life and in the heart, requires the suspension of judgment and striving to be active in truth. Imagine not needing to be concerned with other people, places and things as being right or wrong. Preference didn't exist before given the first opportunity to choose between vanilla or chocolate. Having no preference supposes a neutral attitude with a spark of curiosity. When the basis to make a decision is lacking, trial and error sets the stage to discover what is pleasing and what is not pleasing. One flavor may be more agreeable to the senses than the other. Somewhere along the way, preferences become opinions and the need to look at the menu for new flavors is unnecessary.

Further down the path opinions gain value. Once the self identifies an opinion, the need to defend and guard preferences dismisses the necessity for thinking. The merit of an opinion overpowers the truth. This gives birth to the desire of being right and everything else is wrong. Stepping into judgment is a step away from being present. An unchecked judgment grows in power to enslave and forces the constant, consistent analysis of right or wrong. Lost is the freedom of being present condemned to a prison guarded by staunch conclusions.

A life sentence, it is not. The door to the cell may be opened at any time. Experience relief with the choice to walk away from the responsibility of owning the court room as judge, jury and prosecutor. The invitation is try on the possibility of choosing different perspectives. As the heart opens, the stance on judgment softens. The skills of judgment are good skills. It is the attachment to the judgments that are problematic. Shift the idea that judgment is the only way to form a conclusion. A conclusion comes about through inquiry, logic, conversation, and choices.

Begin considering judgment as a quality of discernment. Discernment requires all the senses to make an assessment. The skill to maintain a flexible attitude does not alter lifestyle. We all maintain certain skills. We know when to wake up in the morning. We know the importance of how and when to apply sunscreen before sitting outside. We know to eat when hungry and drink when thirsty. Think of discernment as a close relative to common sense. The talent for discerning common-sense decisions keeps the body safe and the ego content. The habit to take a complete concept, then break it down into its parts, leads to the discovery of clarity and purpose.

This is a point where love is exploring news of being. This is a time to experience life in a new way. To be aware that moving from one place to another is unsettling for most and the void is overflowing with choice. Be willing to explore various venues to find a suitable expression free of the influence of others.

Courage to Claim Courage

"Courage is the first of human qualities because it is the quality which guarantees the others."

– Aristotle, Philosopher and Polymath

The emergence of courage requires a temporary retreat from the world while gathering information and honing relevant skills. Each experience involving a level of fear builds strength for the next encounter. Bravery is more available each time it is called upon. The things that invoke fear do not go away. Running doesn't place distance between the thing and fear. Everything strikes up fear when fearful. Facing the fear is the only solution.

The resolve to remain the same lingers with the name of that one significant person. The name of that person becomes the excuse to shut down the heart. There are plenty of scenes and a cast of characters that played into the wounded self. Yet all the excuses and all the names reduce themselves to one. The possibility of being anything other than broke, dissolves because of one name. That name is synonymous with the reason one stops showing up. That name is the excuse of why one can't or won't do anything. To face the fear behind that name requires courage – the courage to unlock all the denial associated with that single name. Call courage once, and then again, to gather the strength to step forward.

The step forward to examine what blocks the heart is an exhibition of bravery. Honor the treasure chest's strength and fortitude because the smallest crack brings forth a flood of hurts, wrongs and stuffed emotions. Courage is necessary to reignite the fire in the heart. Fire purges and cleans negative thoughts and hurtful actions. The remnants left from the blaze form the fertile ground in which new growth has a chance to spring forth. Courage requires new tools and a little encouragement to pick them up and use them. Opening the eyes requires courage. Taking a fresh look at dated situations requires courage. Wear courage like new clothes. Answer the question of how it looks and worry not whether it is done right. Fear creates illusion. Courage fades the persistence of an illusion. Courage is what supports the shift through mutable surroundings. Always explore whether that which was true in the mind before the search began remains true now.

Being courageous produces patience. Uncovering resistance is a process that embraces courage and patience. It takes focus and fortitude to build courage. It takes exploration and diligence to understand a problem. It takes inquiry and common sense to find the right solution. It takes effort and calmness to gather the money, the place, the people, and the support. To make a change feels like it takes so much more than what is available. But, in a moment of brilliance and courage, put the idea of well-being first. All the plans, all the solutions, all the requirements stream into that one moment. Breathe deeply and declare life as different. That is courage. Courage resides in the corner of the treasure chest. Dust it off, massage it back to life and kick it into action.

Heart Challenges

"Let us not look back in anger or forward in fear, but around in awareness."

– James Thurber, Writer and Artist

Marking points on the map of self-discovery creates a domino effect. There is no other way than to expect unsuspected upsets to surface and sabotage a quiet peace of mind. There is no hiding from things that bubble up. There is no stuffing the ooze back into a wet paper bag. The container no longer holds all the pieces, it is no longer big enough. The heart and its energy has expanded. Returning to the darkness once light vanquishes the shadows is not an option. Now is the time to gather strength in owning the broken parts. Welcome the choice to seek a better way – a way that is better than the flawed state of any previous existence.

Humans are not textbooks, nor come into this world with instructions. Humans tend to entertain the notion of knowing it all and skim through the list of directions to dismiss seemingly irrelevant tasks and guess which ones are necessary. Following instructions is not easy. Following instructions takes discipline and initiative. Success depends upon moving in the order the steps outline and patience to complete one step at a time. In those moments between here and there, life divides attention. When all is said and done, there remains three different size screws and two washers.

Free will is the practice of roaming a field of choice to pick what best suits the flavor of the day. How that feels to the individual may be utterly different. Separate the word "free" from the notion of "will" for a subjective definition. Thoughts spring forth a sense of freedom or restriction. Will, as a verb, is a passive energy that moves an idea from thought to form. A healthy decision is usually made based on reason or whim. How the decision is made is irrelevant to the importance of accepting the individual responsibility to decide while also supporting others' privilege to do so.

There is a difference between a decision that comes from empowerment to one that is imposed. When the gift of personal power dissolves, choice becomes less of an option. Some people resist making decisions or decide to take the easy way. For them, falling seems easier when pushed down. When getting back up, they have someone else to blame rather than being at fault. Free and willful responsibility is accompanied with consequence. Consequence is the risk of the obvious and not so obvious effects in play before a thing is willed into being.

Ambition is a private endeavor undertaken in the silent folds of the heart. Desire sees the hope of the situation retract when doubt is cast by criticism and dismantled by defeat. During the first moments ambition is challenged, the quiet ego stresses the reasons for caution more clearly than the whispers of the heart's desire. Appease the ego's concern while reinforcing the heart's desire to feed the delicate ambition until determination stands on its own. Appreciate criticism, challenge, and loss as an indication that something is amiss and requires fostering strength and support.

Address criticism, challenge, and loss by drawing a line in the sand with a promise and a heartfelt commitment to never pass this way again. Then, along comes a big wave from the ocean of life to wipe out the line of what was acceptable and erase the history of its making. This indeed feels like starting all over again, but the new starting point contains all the experience, all the lessons, all the wisdom collected to get to this point in the first place. Intentions wash away in a similar way that a label peels from a container when the contents begin to serve a different purpose. The power of observation changes a thing making its convenient label obsolete. A simple observation may erase the line and be the strength needed to move forward.

A label applies to anyone, be they a significant other or life partner, a boyfriend, girlfriend, husband, wife, or spouse and bears a variable weight of responsibility and expectation. Life stories influence the weight, level of indulgence, and the margin of blind acceptance towards a label. History nourishes the future expectations with a label of love that holds the energy of unspoken agreements waiting to be awakened.

The word "love" is both a noun and a verb. Love is the act of affection as well as the object of affection. The object that is loved reflects love. Love expressed looks different for everyone, but the best love is the one that is easy to recognize, calm to embrace, and peaceful to accept. Love energizes when shared and grows when nourished. Without a hint of acknowledgement or a twinkle of reciprocation, doubt tarnishes gratitude. The wheels of judgment begin to grease a slippery slope into a pit of disappointment. Doubt is the forerunner that the quality and quantity of love is in jeopardy. The natural essence of love is to be mutual rather than used as a tool to suffocate one another. The death of a relationship leaves a residue where love once was. Abandoned love continues to seek a form of expression.

Pain happens. A stubbed toe screams for attention and then fades. The stories held about the episode vitalize the suffering. If a story is repeated as sacred or the responsibility for the injury belongs with another, healing is postponed. When the stories cease, and ownership is claimed, the toe is on the mend. A pain-inducing story is a blended combination of variables. Each person involved is a variable, be it they, them, friends, friends of friends, family, me, mine, or ours. Add the histories, upsets, and abuses yours and theirs. The first step to heal or make whole again, is to detach from the perceived source of pain as being something uncontrollable outside our circle of influence. Cut the cord and declare, "whatever another has to do with my sense of well-being be gone." Let go of the perceived value about the infraction. The reaction of letting go is an indicator of progress within the healing process. Let them have their reaction. Attend to any remaining pain of being ignored and abused within the heart center. Know that the other has ignored and abused their heart center as well. Healing begins when a sense of compassion is ignited, first within and then for the other.

Let the heart center come to new terms with expectation by letting go of the desire of wanting to know the outcome of a future event. Conflict occurs when expectations and reality clash in the arena of known and unknown. When left unattended, the level of wanting to know escalates into a hungry, insatiable desire. Desire is not bred in the heart. Desire is the ego's feeling lack and fearing scarcity. Fear of the unknown rests on the doorstep of the heart. Embrace not knowing as a mystery of life. Thriving in not-knowing is a gift. The truth is we know nothing until we know. There is no fear in not-knowing.

Thoughts, words and deeds attract attention as either support or judgment. If that causes the heart to retract from engaging, choose to engage anyway. When doubt and fear come face to face with the heart, choose to face it anyway. The heart automatically resets itself with each return to love. The decision to return to the heart is not always immediate, nor spontaneous. The heart takes time to heal. Reflection supports recalculating a new expression of life. Be patient and persistent. The task to uncompromisingly uncover the dark layers of pain and rejection offers the reward to learn more in how-to expose the true nature of the challenges of the heart.

Breathe into Living

"Breathing is the first act of life, and the last. Our very life depends upon it."

– Joseph Pilates, Inventor of the Art of Contrology and Author

One way to distract pain is to take a deep breath. Love flows with the breath. The inhale and exhale are as significant as the beating of the heart. Draw from the world and give back through the breath. The breath is an offering to the world. Humans are clean-air machines. Mammals draw in oxygen and release carbon dioxide. Plants draw in carbon dioxide and give back oxygen. We are an integral part of the ecological system. Breathing with intent offers an additional dimension of richness to life. Inhale universal peace, exhale a unique brand of peace into the world. The world thrives with every breath offered in love.

The breath is limited when restricted to the upper part of the lungs. Shallow breathing indicates a reserved approach to life. Let the breath be full, deep and complete. Breathe in life. Breathe down into the fingers and toes. Breathe into the heart and muscles. Draw life into the essence of being as if it mattered. When the heart, mind, and belly shuts down, life shuts down. Lower levels of oxygen in the blood depress the state of mind and flattens the line of existence. Breathe deeply with vitality. Breathe life into the body. Breathe life into each experience.

The breath animates the choice of words. When distressed, attempt to verbalize what is the matter. Speak the word, any word, in a way that touches the ear. Let the touch connect with the heart. This is sufficient to take a step back from the upset. Step into a new frontier with each breath. Step away from any habit that hides the hurt. Step into a fresh approach that exposes the hurt. Dance with the breath. Breathing into the area of the wound invites healing.

Breathe and ask the breath to ease the edges of darkness. Let the breath be light. Let the light of life expose the darkness of the self-created tomb. The breath brings possibility and life back to the heart. Light and breath invite hope and reassurance that a new dawn will follow the dark night. Each day that life offers another opportunity to breathe forges the past as a platform to welcome the pending future.

Soften to Grow

"Love is never lost. If not reciprocated,
it will flow back and soften and purify the heart."

– Washington Irving, Writer and Historian

A softened heart incites change and stimulates growth. The request to soften acts as a statement that the current condition is no longer acceptable. Softening implies acceptance for the way things are and a willingness to change. The chunk of coal took years to encase the treasure chest of my heart. Before layers begin to concede, a stream of direct energy needs to break their grip. The nature of the encased treasure chest holds steady and resists change. This is precisely the reason the heart becomes unavailable. Denial feeds the necessity to keep the treasure chest locked. The layers of impenetrable materials are intended to protect against perceived pain. Excavating the layers of protection to get to the heart is risky. What evil lies below? The fear of the unknown paralyzes the effort. The process to unearth the past is sure to awaken the heart to broken and distorted memories.

Acceptance is the initial step into softening the heart. Revitalizing love requires a new consideration of tolerance. This is not a place of defense. Accept and embrace the treasure chest is as it is with a peaceful promise of what may come. The broken pieces build courage. The way to being whole becomes clear with simply receiving our innate gifts, enduring flaws, and necessary disappointments. Then kindly acknowledge that we are all doing the best we can. By accepting this, we are more likely to be accepting of others. Appreciate their dilemma to be exactly who they are in each moment as the world continues to turn. Learning to be a person of acceptance models the way for others. Personal development is not a once-in-a-lifetime event. Personal development is an ever-present, all-encompassing process.

After the acceptance of self, there is pause for the next level of softening. Sitting with the encased heart, there remains hesitation in saying the name. The moment of waiting for a new expression of love hopes to transform the energy that once felt like a punishment. The feeling of love was misplaced. Remember love was identified as rooted in another other than ourselves. The essence of love had depended on circumstances. Love held prisoner, encased in a heart, is love unfulfilled. Love was blind and unaware of what had become of the heart. It was that moment, the moment when another someone asked the question, "Who is the person who holds the key to the silent, cold heart?" The question stirs the heart, but not the answer. The question sparks an interest about the mystery. The question pokes at the excuse for ignoring life and shutting down feelings. The shift is enough space to let the inquiry begin.

When the decision to step away from the pain is made, space is made for opinions to soften. Relaxed opinions no longer anchor one's thoughts to float to the top of the self-generated pool of despair. Step from the cesspool on to firm earth. Rinse away the past and dry off with fresh linen. Stand clean and grounded in a place to release opinions and entertain the possibility to judge less. Judgment can be a foolish misconception of lazy thinking. This type of judgment rarely includes any form of analysis. Conclusions stand strong as thinking escapes. In judgment, the opportunity to examine a situation as good or bad, right or wrong, will or won't, fades. The older the judgment, the less likely the date and circumstance of its origination is remembered. Staunch opinions are a poor substitute for actual thinking.

Life is about enduring the wear and tear directed at the essence of the heart or climbing into a treasure chest to protect the riches of the heart. There comes the time to recall the birthright of innocence. Softening is one key to remembering. Care enough to be that person capable of love. Softening is not a superficial excuse to label any feeling as love. Grow strong to accept the sweet gift to first know, then hold, and ultimately offer the most genuine, authentic love to the world.

Unlock the Heart

"The heart has its prisons that intelligence cannot unlock."

– Marcel Jouhandeau, Writer

When confused, resort to the tools in the treasure chest. One of the most important tools is a fresh pair of glasses. These glasses are prescribed to see beyond the obvious. This is an opportunity to see things in a different light. The glasses may be as simple as wondering what's happening or as complex as revealing in certainty.

"How else can I view the current situation so that
the message I need for my growth comes forth?
What do I need to understand about myself so that I
am free of this confusion?"

The glasses may connect to a higher source and come as a
prayer.

"Help me stop what I am doing that keeps me stuck.
Don't let me return to wrapping my heart in layers
of silent desperation. Let me stay free. My heart, my
treasure chest, and my peace are important to me.
Thank you."

Be open to what happens next. Scan the four energetic
bodies in search of a physical sensation, an emotional
feeling, a mental pressure, or etheric intuition. Ask the
sensation, feeling, or pressure if it relates to something
more painful, seeded deeper in the heart. If the sensation
lives in the heart, let it begin to crack open and present
itself from the heart in a loving way. Let go of what is
happening and the need to know. The need to understand is
less important than the need to let go. Refresh the view,
once, twice, three times. Listen.

Years lapsed after my initial awakening of the heart. I
became familiar with the way my heart contemplated the
world. Being more open and sensitive to my usual musings,
I felt a new sensation. I questioned if the stirring was an old
sensation experienced in a new way, but this felt like a
gigantic pressure as a monumental block of conflicted

direction. I swerved between the desire to be insightful and the urge to resist.

I was in church when I distinctly asked the pressure to share with me what was going on. The pressure dropped into my heart. This was a confirmation that my softened heart was available to help me in a loving way. In that moment, my ears heard the words of the priest and my heart saw the innocence of the children sitting in the pews. I was motionless within an energy springing from the ritual of mass. The hymns tugged at my soul in such a way I was ready to burst. I was afraid of what my shattered heart might look like in the silence of the church, so I attempted to delay the process. I was aware enough to know something was happening and yet afraid of letting my heart explode. I expected the discomfort to reveal itself as tears streaming down my face. The desire to be a total expression of love in unconditional ways became manifest. How many times have I cried because I denied my heart the opportunity to come into its own full expression? How many times had I not listened to the sorrow of my heart and ignored my own growth? I recognized that my heart center was impressing upon me the importance to pay attention now. I took a deep breath as I let the feeling consume me. I allowed my love to express itself. In that moment, I felt the pressure in my heart rise from my chest to my head. The pressure of my heart softened. The pressure in my brow summoned the beginning of the journey into a new realm of transparency.

So be it. When the perception of the world is ugly and unforgiving, don't stop holding the door open for being more humane and kind. Hold steady to be the best loving self as the ultimate model for others to learn and follow. Once the layers and restrictions clear, access to a tool box is granted. The heart center is the home of the treasure chest. From here, re-establish innocence with newfound courage. Call upon the heart's energy and light in a refined art of being. The mind is the next new frontier.

THE MIND

"Great minds discuss ideas, average minds discuss events, small minds discuss people."

– Eleanor Roosevelt, Diplomat and Activist

Now I understood why the cause for my emptiness in the heart was symbolized as a chunk of coal. The coal encased the treasure chest for its own protection. Passage of time and careful observation made it safe for the layers of resistance to peel back and reveal the treasure chest of gifts and tools. Many approaches offer themselves to do this task. When overwhelmed, the better approach may be pause. Courage is a prerequisite to step forward to bring light into darkness. Courage aids the development of a personal sense to be present in each moment through the practice of bringing value to feelings. If the heart is the center of feeling, then what is the center of the mind? There is nothing inherent about the brain that suggests it "thinks." This is not a conversation about the intelligence of being. This is about exploring the function of the mind center as it best serves the understanding of ourselves.

Walking through life is the act of placing one foot in front of the other in such a way that the obstacles on the path are manageable. The mind remains engaged until the attention is disrupted with a preoccupation to trail toward a seemingly more interesting arena. That path is littered with bottomless potholes. Boredom and whimsey speckle the path to distract and test one's character. The mind shifts between intense focus, creating significance, or managing the requests of other people and places. The force of distraction increases with the demand to remain the same.

When the struggle to comprehend overwhelms peace of mind, the tendency to accept things as perceived feels easier than to seek the allusive truth. Acceptance breathes freshness into exhausting situations. Yes, acceptance is a skill of the heart, and of the mind as well. A confused mind craves information and will haphazardly assign meaning and significance to the trivial. Managing all this mind stuff begs for an additional skill that comes to mind, that is the ability to learn and retain.

Think, Learn, and Retain

"I think, therefore I am."

– René Descartes,
Philosopher and Scientist

Every thought I entertain about the course of thinking appears in the form of a question. What is the true function of the brain? Is it to think, to learn, or to retain? Does any of this serve a purpose or is it an excuse to fill time? What is this thing called "thinking" anyway? Do answers lie within? Or fresh ideas come from the ethers? Do ideas appear when rummaging through old files of memories to create something new? Are thoughts original, something received, or recalled? And where are all these "thinks" stored?

What is it about the brain that indicates it "thinks?" Thinking is not of the brain or attributed to any one organ. Where does thought originate? If thinking is an activity of the brain, ask the heart about its thoughts. Does feeling include thinking about feelings? Does the brain think the body is hungry or does the belly shout out, "Feed me!" And then the rest of the body responds with a sympathetic impulse, yes. Ask any part of the body a question and receive a response.

Careless thinking leaves little room for new material to come in to play. In this crazy, always doing something world, the comfort of silence is foreign. When asked to quiet the mind, the mind scrambles to search for the easiest way to become silent. The attempt to create stillness becomes quite loud. A fight ensues between thoughts of inability and resistance to make sure the mind remains busy. The upset may originate from the ego because silence threatens the ego's dominion.

Quieting the mind becomes an art form. A quiet mind is the prerequisite for learning. Judgments, opinions, and expectations disguise themselves as a valuable product of learning. The best learning occurs with the suspension of judgment and invitation to curiosity. Let the world be the classroom to receive new information, or at least be open to receiving. A personal agenda that includes expectations is a form of distraction. Expectations spin around in wonder of what's going on. Learning becomes the victim to the teacher. Entering the classroom to learn is different for everyone. Some minds need a moment to purge chummy distractions, while other minds are ready to start.

Readiness may stumble when redirected from the start. The test of mental flexibility is how quickly the mind returns to the point when asked to deviate from the original purpose. When detached from expectations, thoughts are more likely to glide between topics. A distraction acts like a zip line for the attention to slip away from the current and comfortable place to rummaging through past experiences searching for a semblance of safety. Some minds can jump between here and there, while other minds need time to process. Either way, energies shift in the form of composure to return to the purpose at hand.

The energy of mentally engaging inquiry, research, and communication is not the same. There are different kinds of teaching and diverse ways of retention based on a learning style of hearing, seeing, or doing. The individual may respond more quickly and greater one way, but awareness of all types is beneficial.

One more little thought about the function of the mind as a storehouse of processes and depot of views, feelings and emotions. Ask the mind a question. Where is the workshop, the place that holds the inventory of resources to create thinking and maintains the archives of solutions? Where is the repository of past problems? Is this stored in a single place? Does it feel like a blind walk through the halls of the mind, searching for the right room that houses the file cabinet of life? There is no single answer, only the wonder – while musing over memories, pondering problems and searching solutions. Each thought potentially holds a charge, be it one of comfort or discomfort.

If a word, thought, or situation stimulates a response, notice where in the body the charge appears. A quick and knee jerk reaction may be around the heart, the shoulder blades, or the throat. The charge indicates something significant has yet to be resolved. The onset hints at the charge's nature of love, betrayal, or fear. Following the charge offers choice each step of the way during this exercise of learning, action, or yielding to the stimulus.

Discerning Minds

"It is the mark of an educated mind to be able to entertain a thought without accepting it."

– Aristotle, Philosopher and Student of Plato

The heart, mind, and belly together contribute to the core. The mind center supports gathering and categorizing experiences, memorizes thoughts and feelings, and collects, analyzes, and formulates results and conclusions.

The mind is recognized for its decision-making ability. Each decision leaves a trace of its outcome as a tie that binds it to the memory. An evidence trail remains for easy access to recall any detail of the memory when necessary. The mind, in conjunction with the ego, holds the ability to act in ways to offend or avoid offense. The mind discriminates sensitive data from private information. Each person is a collection of information deposited in the world to make a difference. The value is in the interest attached to the wealth of knowledge. When it is time to take the next step, or generate a sensible decision, we each have our own resource library available to consult.

Discernment is valuable as an asset. The mind that discerns well, also investigates in a fair and logical manner. The fear of losing the mind through dementia or head trauma stifles the imagination of how anyone can continue living with the loss of a rational mind. An irrational mind wanders conflicted through a collection of nothing. There is no inkling to what it is like to no longer know or even care to know likes and dislikes. Imagine the mind riding the waves of unrelated, random stimuli. The need for interaction drowns beneath the undercurrent. The functioning mind strives to silence the demented information of its deafening emptiness. Clear is this possibility that clear thinking can turn out to be "mumble-jumbled." That is, if not already present. The ransacked library leaves behind an arbitrary, disorganized pile of nothingness. All its content is long overdue because the context is irrelevant. All that remains is a fleeting yarn for a functioning mind to fill gaps and straighten out inconsistencies.

The mind without a valid thought system is reduced to weigh the value of things one of two ways, either as good or bad, right or wrong, black or white. Such binary thoughts offer no shades of gray. Such thinking limits choice to this or that and never the possibility of both. The mind essentially operates as a pendulum. Thoughts pass through gradients of gray between the extremes of black and white. The two settings of on and off limit the decision-making process. Aspects of the personality harden and the ability to go with the flow slows down. Although a diagnosis of dementia or a brain trauma is nonexistent, life is no better off. This is something we do to ourselves. The burden to be the best judge and most efficient jury, reduces the necessity to entertain questions from the prosecutor or defense attorney. The mind has decided, and the world becomes predictable and mundane. The decision to change the situation requires the effort to step from behind the judge's bench and let precious judgments take a holiday. Let opinions unwind into preferences and certainty ease into discernment. This place of ease encourages the enjoyable act of gathering as much information as available. Thoughts then come from a place of wisdom.

Being open to discern is an action that invigorates the gift of intuition. When the process to determine the next best step takes too long, it is convenient to revert to whatever worked. Comprehension, adjustment, intuition and trust, all have a role to play in discernment. Confidence grows in the ability to follow an inclination through fruition. Practice doesn't ensure the intuition improves or that more reliable perceptions are received. This is a case where the skills of intuition are not a destination but requires attention. When the reliability of information is questionable, trust that something can be known without knowing it as fact.

David and Goliath

"If I have seen further it is by standing on the shoulders of Giants."

– Isaac Newton, Mathematician

The day I sat on the pew, in the church, I accepted my heart as willing to open in new ways to experience love. The familiar pressure of knowing my heart elevated to an unfamiliar sensation in my brow. I instantaneously intuited the pressure signaled that now was the time to examine an open mind. I likened this moment to that initial feeling in my heart of a hardened chunk of coal protecting an encrusted treasure chest. As my heart had hardened to protect itself, my mind followed its lead.

The pressure in my brow felt immense. I asked the pressure that if it could take a form, what form would it be? The question massaged the pressure into an image of a sleeping giant. The giant was big, strong, and captured my attention. I asked the pressure again, please let me see a way to understand the gigantic pressure behind my brow. Like a dream, the question revealed that the answer comes from the story of David and Goliath. I asked again if the message wasn't Jack and the Bean Stalk? What was it about the story of David and Goliath that could offer an understanding about the nature of this pressure at my brow?

The story of David and Goliath comes from the Old Testament, the history of the Jewish people. King Saul and the Israelite's were at war with the Philistines. The two armies were at an impasse in the Valley of Elah. Elah is a metaphysical symbol of oak and strength, and the valley would be the division between the two. One Philistine soldier named Goliath sustained the impasse. Goliath stood on the floor of the valley for forty days and forty nights. Each morning and every evening, Goliath challenged the Israelite soldiers to fight him. If Goliath won the fight, the Israelites' would become the Philistines' slaves. In return, if Goliath lost, the Philistines would become the Israelites' servants.

Goliath was a mean-looking, loud, giant. No member of King Saul's army volunteered to fight the giant. A young shepherd boy, David, felt a sense of duty and stepped forward to challenge the giant. David was a good shepherd. Once, while protecting the flock of lambs, David had killed a lion. Another time he killed a bear, both by using his slingshot. In his innocence, David believed he could end the impasse. David believed his skills of protecting sheep could protect the soldiers. What he did with the lion and the bear could be just as effective against the Palestine giant.

King Saul was at a loss. He believed he had no alternative. The only thing King Saul could do for David was to offer his armor to wear as protection. Saul was a big man compared to David, who was but a youth. The set of armor was too big for David. The armor would only get in his way. David walked into battle with his shepherd's staff and his slingshot. He picked up five stones from the bank of the stream and placed them in a bag tied at his waist. The outraged Goliath sneered at the boy who would bring a stick to do battle. Goliath lumbered toward David. David placed one of the five stones in his sling, whirled it over his head, and released it. The stone hit Goliath's forehead and the giant fell. David took Goliath's own sword to behead him. The standoff was over.

What was it about this story I needed to understand? Was it that I was in a valley, a low point, struggling to get back to a higher ground? The pressure at my brow was more distinct. I considered Goliath as an archetype for the human ego and the sheep herder as an innocent caretaker of a flock of rogue thoughts. The five stones may represent the five senses or the body, feelings, memories, free will, and nature. The bag where David held the stones is a container representing the ego's desire. What of the beheading? Was this a matter of separating the head from the body, or my thinking from my feeling? Did I need awakening with a swift and powerful strike to my brow? Was I to receive a spiritual truth or challenge my faith to disrupt old thought? Which aspect of me did I need to call on for this task? Was it my body, my feelings, my memories, free will or the desire of my ego?

Then There's This

"David should have killed Goliath with a harp."

– Stanislaw Lec, Philosopher and Satirical Poet

Author Malcolm Gladwell shared his insights about David and Goliath in a TED Talk published in September, 2013. Mr. Gladwell explained that in those times, armies consisted of three units; cavalry, infantry, and artillery. The most populated group of soldiers was the infantry whom engaged in hand to hand combat. The cavalry doesn't participate in this story. The artillery used slings, not sling shots, to propel objects at their enemy. The handheld slings were accurate up to 200 yards away from the battle. Stones coming from a sling moved at a speed of close to 100 miles per hour.

Goliath was abnormal. He stood tall at six-foot, nine-inches. Goliath may have suffered from acromegaly, which is a hormonal disorder that occurs when the pituitary gland produces too much growth hormone. The hormone also affects vision. Goliath needed to be led to the battle because he couldn't see well. Goliath was slow in his actions and reactions. He couldn't make out who David was. He couldn't identify him as a young boy. Goliath could not make out the difference between a stick and a shepherd's staff. Goliath thought he saw a stick. This insulted him, that this was the weapon of choice brought to defeat him. And Goliath did not see the stone coming toward his forehead.

The parts of the story that speak to me are the giant, the stone, and the shepherd's innocence. These felt relevant to the opening of the mind. The giant is symbolic of a buildup of huge pressure caused by resistance. I did not question the pressure. I resigned myself to ignore the invisible resistance as part of my daily routine. The mere presence of the giant invoked fear in the soldiers. The mere presence of the pressure behind my brow held me from engaging in my own battle of life. Things large and unknown tend to rattle the way of being. The inclination is to fall back to sleep because it is easier to slumber than take up arms for battle. David chose a sling and a single stone at close range to bring down this obstacle and end the standoff. This story is indicative of every battle when the sense of self is divided in two.

When confronted with an obstacle, which one of the five stones in the bag hits the mark? Is it the physical body, feelings, thoughts, or memories that serve? Is it by free will, or resorting to follow the whims of the ego? Is it a single stone aimed at the middle of thoughts and judgments to startle the intuition? Is it best to surrender false judgments rather than test short-lived inclinations? If higher levels of understanding begin to take form, does fear source retreat? The power of a single stone can break through an obstacle. Physically, mentally, or emotionally, when the soft spot is struck, the giant falls. David, the innocent shepherd, was young and naive. David was completely focused on the task at hand. David's innocence kept him from actualizing his fear. His motivation came from a sense of responsibility. David aimed his service for a greater good.

The biblical version of the story implied the giant as evil. The giant was a victim of his circumstance. He was big, confused, and his vision impaired what he saw as different from what the other soldiers on the field saw. He was not a member of the infantry nor artillery. He was a giant doing what a giant does. Then, this outsider, this non-soldier, this shepherd boy, broke the standoff. David's skill that kept sheep safe in their fields brought down the giant. The giant represents a state of being asleep. David refused to accept the reality held by all the other soldiers that nothing was possible. They resolved to repeat the same scenario, rather than change. Surrendering to the situation and doing nothing seemed the safest option. The perception was that the giant was the symbol of what kept the opposing soldiers afraid and silent. But, David was not a soldier.

Consider the giant's fall as symbolic of a rough awakening. The elements of the story include the giant, the soldiers, the shepherd, the sling, and the kings. Stories generally include an element that suggests sleep and tranquility as a viable solution. Everyone in the Bible story was willing to wait. Everyone that is, except David. The movement of one, small element acted as a catalyst to initiate change. This is the time when new doors open, like the wakening of insight. When awakened from a deep sleep, all the senses rise to a higher level of operation.

The giant knew nothing more than to accept his fate within the current situation. The soldiers on both sides of the valley had nothing to gain from being a hero. Let someone else volunteer rather than take a chance to alter the situation. And then the fearless young boy David, stepped forward.

Saul was the first king of the Israelites, appointed by God. Saul represented power and all that was right. The people loved Saul until he grew weak and his power diminished. After King Saul died, the adult shepherd-boy, David became king. Saul personified power. David was the heart of love. The king who followed David, King Solomon, epitomized wisdom.

The bible tells stories of David, riding the waves of all types of love. The story of David and the giant is the power of love at its most innocent. The story of David and his obsession for the wife of one of his soldiers, is the destructive nature of love. David had the husband assigned to the front line of battle, never to return home again. Love operates as a filter for the mind to perceive the world. When in a life battle, the effort is to see a thing in full context or at least enhance the ability to see things differently. Once all the thoughts of what to do have been done, wait and call on blind faith to show what and where to go next. Gather courage to ask how to think about those gigantic feelings. And how to move through and beyond any mental pressure of resistance.

Tools of the Mind

"Wisdom is your perspective on life, your sense of balance, your understanding of how the various parts and principles apply and relate to each other. It embraces judgment, discernment, comprehension. It is a gestalt or oneness, and integrated wholeness."

– Stephen R. Covey, Author and Motivational Speaker

The heart center's tools clean and clear to illuminate the energy of love. The lightness of the heart can shift its focus from the act of doing to the state of being. As the ego befriends the heart, the heart summons courage to face and challenge anything less than being content.

The tools of the mind differ from that of the heart. The mind develops tools to gather and withdraw value from information. The mind weighs the stimulus against the response to form a conclusion. The results collected from this formula have been passed down through generations. The stories stay the same, but the names and the characters change. Each generation upgrades their personalities to reflect modern discoveries. What may have been territories is now neighborhoods. The way to move around was horse and carriage is now horsepower and automobile. And the reaction to scandal may have softened or not.

The mind is about ideas, knowledge, and conscience. All things are perfect in its ideal state until it takes form. Forms and systems are subject to deterioration. Once a system is in place, it is imperfect. A good idea that happened yesterday is still a good idea today and has endured the test of 24 hours. That is plenty of time to form an opinion. From one generation to the next is enough time for the value of an opinion to change and morals to evolve.

People tend to settle in their ways when not challenged. The current place is good if not pushed or thrown into new situations. Systems, when not exercised, become hardened. Morals shift as humanity matures. Moving from "must have" to a personal preference broadens the selection of options. Consumerism is an example that thrives with the increased number of choices. Choice keeps the buyer engaged if not at least guessing. When the chains that bind us to yesterday have been broken the reward is choice. When the past is remembered as not good enough, the motivation to remain open is more likely. There are those who can go along or strive to expand the menu of preferences. The nature of a growing mind is to take a chance on experiencing something new. Life is more pleasant when surrounded by those who are open to experience new things. Be that person.

A judgment is based on facts, samples, details and proof. A judgment may be more of an informed decision. Holding fast to judgments, however, stifles growth. When our system is sound and established, having a strong sense of good judgment is something to be proud of. Having good judgment is different from being a good judge. Having good judgment is a quality of being that person from whom others seek advice or counsel. The best decisions come from wisdom coupled with discernment. Being independent of concrete opinions, offers freedom to volley challenges as appropriate. We are not our opinions. When opinions become rooted in identity, judgment can't discern or even entertain what is best. A judgment left unquestioned, tested by time, hardens into a grudge. Grudges feed feelings of resentment, grief, and bitterness. When left unattended, grudges cast a shadow on the library of thoughts and memories. Until there is willingness to turn away from darkness, the ability to soften views is limited. The reconciliation of differences permits the gentle application of the salve of forgiveness.

A few people ponder the importance and direction of society's moral and ethical system. It is a rare occurrence if every member of the same family shares similar values. A sense of morals and ethics comes from the sense of a greater purpose. A population accepts and operates within a margin around its code of conduct. The moral and ethical system supports the establishment of rules around the margin. The goal of a judicial system is to be fair and applicable for all individuals. A stable system is when everyone follows the same rules, in the same way, that is good for the whole of society.

Meeting of Minds

"It is every man's obligation to put back into the world at least the equivalent of what he takes out of it."

– Albert Einstein, Physicist and Founder of the Theory of Relativity

Life is about making connections. The significance of a day is greater than the brief, courteous small-talk exchanges that accumulate from the multitude of mindless greetings. The possibility of meaningful interaction requires effort. The worn-out script of words held in our cadre of sayings of which one is drawn to toss out at another, is not a conversation, let alone a connection. It is an obligatory rhetorical question put forth with little regard for a response.

Usually words carry a sentiment and the flow of words is a bridge between the speaker and the listener. Communication is knowing that an expressed pattern of words met its mark as received. Communication is a form of relationship. There are relationships that transcend time and words. No matter the words, each other understands what is being said. There are relationships that won't, don't, and will never make any sense. Sometimes the words cannot make themselves heard regardless of the volume they carry.

Not all factors need to be the same for minds to meet. Minds don't need to be the same age, nor share the same life experiences. The meeting is not exclusive to gender or race. Those involved in meeting do not have to match in any way. The mind serves best when it comes from a place of curiosity. For the curious mind, there are no dead ends, only temporary detours. Curiosity is not restricted because interest feeds upon the unknown. The mind is boundless in the company of like minds as they nourish each other. The meeting embraces encouragement, respect, and inquiry. The exchange of words is a playful volley aimed at keeping the interaction alive. The meeting takes a wrong turn when an opinion becomes a weapon, rather than a bridge. Opinion becomes a personal attack when aimed to maim a trusted certainty within the other's belief system.

There are instances that a relationship welcomes playing on a dangerous field of adversity. Insults are fun until a wound is inflicted. The reply is that it was only a joke. The mind withdraws and learns to avoid land mines and maneuvers around obstacles. Clashing of minds offers a different type of excitement than the meeting of minds. Minds do not meet when shields of defense activate. Attitudes of superior and inferior affect the playing field as being uneven and slippery. Those participating in a bicker party of sorts begin to cast blame and entertain doubt for fun. Hits and misses tally up with the winner taking the spoils and leaving behind their disregarded civility that dismantled future relations. In this match, there are no sacred boundaries. Any line of decency is a marked target. Skewed lines served with a demand to be right hold little regard for happiness. There are no winners in this battle of minds, only losers.

Beyond the Mind

*"Our mind is capable of passing beyond the dividing line
we have drawn for it. Beyond the pairs of opposites of
which the world consists, other, new insights begin."*

– *Hermann Hesse, Novelist and Painter*

Living a full life suggests there exists a point established for something perceived as true, like true North on a compass. If the aim is to be at peace, raise the sails with an intention for a peaceful passage. Set the course by using the compass and map the voyage clear of known dangers. Wait for a gentle breeze to rise. The North Pole's magnetic properties attracts the magnetic needle of the compass as intention attracts peace. The winds adjust to support the aim when clear. Winds stir the sails, yet the direction of movement remains unpredictable. Any departure in the course caused by the shifting wind can be managed, yet a steady eye holds on to the desired course. There is no better way to navigate an appreciation of peace than by experiencing a disruption. The lesson is in being able to drift away from peace as calmly as possible until a return to the original course. Challenges reveal the depth of the commitment to be peaceful.

Straying off course into uncharted waters stifles the ability to predict the unknown. When cast into a situation created by another, there is little room for error in getting back on track. Returning to the intended course requires diligence and strength. Hunkering down is contrary to the idea of going with the flow. This is not giving up. This is a mental shift set to accommodate other ways of problem solving. Stay true to the course until it no longer serves the intention for obtaining the highest good.

The course shifts when others force a different outcome. That is time to question, whom does this journey serve? All journeys are subject to distractions. Question the distractions. Don't deviate from the course by following smoke when looking for the fire. Follow smoke all the way to the flame, rather than track the evasive way the wind blows. The smoke is an effect. The problem is the thing that is on fire. Ask the mind to study the details. Determine the best course of action to uncover the cause and return to the flow of a peaceful mindset.

Aim to understand the mind while attempting to understand others. Detach from a situation, for the space to make sense of what is controlling thoughts and decisions. Clear the smoke, but don't rely on the most dramatic symptom as being the root cause. Understanding a situation is easier when attempting to grasp the fullness of what is happening by accepting as much information as possible. Consider all its variables; people, places, things, history, goals, and purpose when applicable. Widen the exploration with a net fully open to capture an array of variables. This is stepping beyond the physical into the mental realm of the four-energy body model.

Beyond the mind is the world where every person is unique. In that realm awaits the gifts of the visionary or intuitive. That territory is safe to experiment with the limitless contributions as a sensitive or empath. Natural senses, when asked, expand their capabilities. Take the time to recognize pain and suffering or pleasure and comfort as it is true for others. Empathy is one step deeper in living the feeling as the other does. Accept all forms of ourselves as mental, emotional, and sensitive beings. Standing on the platform, be willing to leap beyond the physical realm. If we are called to be of any kind of service, it is imperative to mentally assess the feelings from the heart. By first knowing and owning our feelings, then the skill increases to sense feelings being sourced elsewhere. To feel the feelings of another is to do so in a different way. Feel the feelings of others without having intimate knowledge of the cause of the feeling. Know thyself first because the encounter with a foreign feeling is like stepping onto a cloud of confusion.

Some empaths have psychic abilities. The psychic empath recognizes the gap between themselves and another. They know they are not the source and they know to identify the feeling as coming from elsewhere. The psychic empath frees themselves from the source's pain and suffering. Pain is real, suffering is a choice. There are people who wish not to deal with suffering. They are comfortable handing the suffering off to someone else. The person experiencing the suffering chooses how long and in what form to continue. The empath sends healing to the painful situation with an intention for a greater good. The healing floats about in the ethers waiting for the person to end their suffering and accept healing.

It is prudent for people to know the difference between sympathy and empathy. The sympathizer feels the energy coming from sadness and pity and then moves on. The empath experiences the suffering of the world. Torment pokes at the empath because the source of the suffering is a mystery. Not knowing the source of suffering is suffering in and of itself. The search for the source and the suffering, allows no room for anything other than anguish. The empath learns to stand in the narrow gap between the self and the suffering open to the answer of the question to whom does this belong. The empath begins to cultivate the grounds of suffering into a source of healing and growth. The act to transform suffering into nourishment is underway. Heal the suffering with a regimen of light and energy. The ability to acknowledge and release suffering fulfills the purpose of healing.

Obstacles of the Mind

"Obstacles cannot crush me. Every obstacle yields to stern resolve. He who is fixed to a star does not change his mind."

– Leonardo da Vinci, Renaissance Polymath

The heart responds when it feels assaulted by thoughts, words, or deeds. Moments of doubt and fear, loss and disappointment, keeps the mind from engaging the heart.

Hurt demands attention. The heart corrects itself by returning its focus to love. Healing is not a matter of taking the time to think, plan, and decide how to proceed. Healing occurs as a matter of opening the door and proclaiming it is so.

The mind collects information and files it for future reference. Being caught in the trap of circular thinking stops the search for new information. The mind perceives stalling as an obstacle in how to manage new, incoming information. If the information doesn't sync with the current thought process, then the moment expands to accommodate digestion. Some minds have a robust information management system able to handle different information with the same success every time. The receipt of information gets a stamp of approval or rejected as unnecessary. Ideally, the mind remains neutral with a tendency toward gratitude or doubt. A grateful mind is more likely to see possibility while the doubtful mind hesitates and ruminates.

When doubt turns inward and feeds upon itself, darkness spreads. Doubt is personal and focuses on blame. In the darkness, the fault lies within, not with the information. The mind ruminates on questions of why and what. "Why am I like this?" Isn't it possible that beyond human error is the chance for incorrect information or misleading interpretation leading in a wrong direction?

Hesitation signals the time is right to ask the ego its role in the decision-making process. When a decision is accompanied by internal pressure, the chance is high that the ego is protecting an opinion. When the mind continues to seek a better solution, the operation behaves in a more open way. When agitated, the mind becomes energized like a thunderstorm. Step into the storm. Invite the clouds to open. Let it pour. When thoughts plummet in a dreadful spiral, release the feeling. Be like a top and let it spin to its resting place. When there is certainty that the mind is working overtime, step back, pause, and ask for a fresh way to regard the situation.

Calm the Mind

"Nothing is so bitter that a calm mind cannot find comfort in it."

– Seneca, Philosophy and Statesman

We already know all the ways to calm ourselves. As a youngster, we learned to soothe ourselves with a blanket or a favorite toy. We may have soothed ourselves with food or sleep. As we get older, we chose other habits that may have been more harmful than good.

The choice on how to become calm is a personal one. There is no need to understand why something works or doesn't work. The moment effort is exerted to figure out why, the endless maze of thinking returns. At this point, don't squander effort in an exercise of failure, but rather success. Resort to the things known to work. The thinking mind thrives on variety. As a refresher, consider these nine ways to calm the mind that are better than creating bad habits.

Read If current affairs disturb thoughts, then reading the newspaper will not be a source of peace. Even the comics illustrate dark places within current events. There are books that offer a positive thought a day. Redirect thinking with the nudge of a simple, single word. Such books exist to encourage constructive thinking, observe religious views, or support an inclusive world view. Books that inspire an optimistic outlook, clear the mind and returns a sense of well-being.

Write Keep a notebook handy. Use the page to dive into a bothersome issue. Start with a list of happy things. Gratitude acts as a reminder that all is not bad. The power gained when capturing thoughts on paper is limitless. To be able to articulate the problem requires the mind to wrap itself completely around it. Being able to see what is going on allows the freedom to decide what is important or frivolous. When the search for the reason of a puzzle feels like beating the head against a wall, then it is time to stop and step away from the wall. Come back to what is good in life. Read the list of thankful things or generate a new list of happiness. List the things that make the world good. Start the list with air, water, and then add more personal things. Take a moment to look outside the window or walk in nature. Take a moment to look inside. Find something to hold onto, something that is good.

Quiet Meditation is a form of quieting the mind. The word meditation elicits an array of emotions from hip-hip-hooray to nay. The complaint about meditation is that it takes too much time or is too difficult. Any preconceived thoughts about meditation will put a stop before getting started. The word meditation has an energetic charge. The attempt to neutralize charged thoughts about meditation usually ends in a mental scuffle. There is still merit in quieting the mind. Clear out contemporaneous chatter for room to contemplate a stance on an issue. Before asking the mind to visualize or rest, let the body lead the way by choosing either to sit or lie down. Sitting keeps the mind alert and lying lets the body relax. Sitting may be uncomfortable but lying down invites sleep. Try both ways. Once the body settles, let the mind follow. Think about a topic or let all thoughts fall away with the purpose to become calm. Don't fight with the thoughts, don't try to ignore or discredit the activity. By acknowledging the thought, it is free to float away. In the process, check in with the heart for its notion about what is good for the mind.

Breath work The body is amazing. Physical functions tend to happen automatically. Breathing is one such thing likely to be taken for granted. Our first act as a human on this earth is to take in a breath and our last act is to exhale. In between the two is life.

> Humans tend to shorten or even hold their breath. Breathing through the nose calms the body. The cycle of breath begins with a complete exhale until all the air is pushed from the body. Then, allow the

body to deeply draw in the breath as if it were the first. There are four important parts to each breath. The inhale and exhale are apparent. The not so apparent parts are the active pauses between the two. The breath doesn't switch on and off between inhale and exhale. The breath flows through a subtle shift from inhale to exhale and exhale to inhale. Not a stop and go, but a flow of air moving through the body. The focus to breathe deeply, quiets the mind.

Music Sound stimulates and soothes. Quiet the mind by comforting the auditory senses. There are two forms of sound that quiet the mind, the rhythmic style of music and the calming acoustics of the word. Music may offer greater results in less time than meditation. Sound, through music or meditation, directs the mind's attention away from itself. Music interrupts the routine of thinking.

Talk As ears hear, the mouth speaks. Like a teapot, speaking lets off steam. The release of internal pressure gives way to a fresh opportunity to think. The ideal person to hear another's words is the one who is not full of their own ideas and solutions. If that person is not available, then start an internal dialogue. Ask the mind open-ended questions with answers beyond a simple yes or no. Be patient and listen to hear the reactions formed as words or experience a response from the body.

Exercise No one exercise is better than another and no one exercise meets everyone's needs. The best exercise is the one that suits needs and goals. The best exercise is the one that brings joy when the body moves. The best exercise comes with excitement as the energy returns to a natural flow. Joy and excitement can happen while one is walking or practicing yoga. Joy and excitement can happen while running or lifting weights. Movement can be thoughtless or thought-filled. Moving the body frees the mind, or at least opens a gap to let in fresh ideas.

Affirmations Positive thinking isn't for everyone. A positive thought slapped over a gaping wound of negativity doesn't make the pain go away. Positive thinking does not work when avoiding a pain filled memory.

Creating an affirmation is tricky. Some words propose lack and other words presume the presence of lack. The word "want" suggests lacking the thing being desired. The word "enough" hints of something more than what is. Some words exist because of its opposite. "Love" is not the opposite of "hate." "Ignorance" is not the opposite of "bliss." But then, the word "positive" is because of its opposite word "negative". A positive affirmation is only effective after all layers of doubt have been neutralized.

Consider an affirmation as separate from being the activity of positive thinking. The power of the affirmation is its underlying suggestion. An effective affirmation is not intended to cover up the feeling of lack. An effective affirmation stands on its own as if true now. An affirmation is a declaration of the current state "I" as being true regardless of what is going on in other parts of life.

Start with a goal in mind. Generate a list of thoughts that support this goal. Remove all the mental objects that use negative words that suggest lack, such as "no," "not," or "never." Review the list of thoughts that support the goal and select two or three that feel good. Write them down and keep them handy. Repeat them often with confidence. Say the affirmation until it is so. Then, create a new affirmation to support a new goal.

Re-frame Reframing is a simple shift in how something is seen by minimizing any charge that arises to view the thing in a different light. Once a worrisome thought grabs hold, it is hard to let the distraction go. Consider that a different point of view may reveal that the original thought isn't all it was thought to be. Get a feeling for the type of thought it is. By type, classify it as a worry, fear, avoidance, anxiety, or any flavor between. Label the thought by its type. Bringing attention to the belief changes the nature of the thought. The thought may intensify or decrease. Let the label evolve to reflect the changing nature of the thought as it pretends to be okay or tries to get away and hide. Make sure the label continues to name the thought until the thought pattern has cleared. Part of the thought pattern is that it appears as a victim. An external stimulus triggers a response at the target the victim holds. Identifying how the trigger works can clarify the type of thought. When there is a better understanding of its type and its trigger, options open. Start to construct a new frame around an old photo. Now it appears as not so bad possibilities instead of the debilitating story. Time to start the process to detach from irrelevant and extraneous thinking.

Mind Feeds Belly

"Your beliefs become your thoughts,
Your thoughts become your words,
Your words become your actions,
Your actions become your habits,
Your habits become your values,
Your values become your destiny."

– Mahatma Gandhi, Antiwar Activist

What comes to mind with the words "food for thought?" The quality of thought affects the body. When held too long, thoughts grow roots like a weed. Holding thoughts show up in different parts of the body. The thoughts that don't pass through, create an energetic blockage. At first the blocks appear as an annoyance, then an ache or pain. At best, the aches and pains capture the attention and demand action to clear the energy out of the body by calming the mind or changing the attitude. At worst, the physical system adjusts into discomfort and dis-ease. We accept more than we believe we can handle. When desperate to hold on, exhaustion preys on the unsuspecting. Then it is time to begin the work of letting go. There is always the choice in the matter to dissolve and discharge heavy energy or move the bundle of thoughts through the body. Choose to release the energy and release the body's attraction to the energy.

The natural order is that energy comes into the heart as a feeling. Then, the feeling passes through the mind as a thought. Finally, the thought sinks into and through the belly as an emotion. The thoughts being fed to the mind and nourishing the body do so through its digestive system. As words have power, thoughts have power, too. Thoughts fuel the capability of making decisions and taking actions.

THE BELLY

"The belly rules the mind."

– Proverb

One of Aesop's fables was about the belly and its members. Seems that the members got tired of doing all the work and saw the belly do nothing. The legs carried the body to labor in the fields. The feet walked the body back and forth to the fields. The arms carried the fruits of labor. The hands worked the tools to grow the food and prepare the meals. The mouth held the food while the teeth chewed into bits that were easily swallowed. The members were angry that they did all the work to feed the belly, and the belly did nothing in return. The belly was lazy and contributed nothing. So, they decided to starve the belly by going on strike. They refused to do anything until the belly started working. Only a few days passed as the arms and legs, hands and feet became weak and weary from the lack of food. The members realized that the work the belly did was to keep them healthy and strong. The first thing they did when they came off strike was to feed the belly.

The final center of the four-body model of physical, emotional, mental, and etheric, is the belly. The belly hasn't always been third to the heart and mind. When survival was more of a dominant force in the hierarchy, the belly was the primary go-to center. Humans relied on the belly center to stay alive. Humans have relied on the belly's reactions long before thoughts and feelings became important. Life became complicated when thoughts received greater weight than instincts. Value was added to thoughts as more important, right and wrong, or good and bad. These values were applied to things and relationships. If that is not enough, there are mean and nasty things that happen outside the value scheme. The effects of residual emotions became a topic for analysis and examination. In the age of innocence, the instincts of the belly directed action. Hot, move. Hungry, eat. Tired, sleep. The more civilized the society, the less dependence on the instincts of the belly. Decisions counted more on the feelings of the heart and the thoughts of the mind. "I was treated poorly, I'm running away. I enjoyed that experience, I'll return." By listening to the heart and mind over the instincts of the belly, the belly softened. The intelligence of the belly was silenced.

Think about what important activities relate in some way to the belly. The belly is responsible for turning food into energy to keep the body fueled. The energetic roots of the belly connect to the earth. Located near the digestive system is the reproductive system. Reproductive organs influence how one shows up in the world as man or woman. There is also the energy of identifying as male or female. There is growing tension between camps trying to understand the difference between the actual hardware and the energy in how one self-identifies. The workings of the male or female energies influence how to root being human through the belly. People are being asked to go beyond the physicality of the anatomy. Courageous souls are speaking out about their tension and share how they are coming to terms with it. Masculinity and femininity is the energy of giving and receiving. The masculine energy is active. The feminine is receptive. The belly has a lot more going on than digesting the lunch that the mouth and teeth members provided.

The belly is both masculine and feminine. The belly is the seat of action that receives and digests information to nourish the next move. The fuel created through digestion decides whether to stay right where it is or act. The seat of action, does not act completely on its own. The belly responds to the messages of the heart and the mind. The heart is the seat of love, the mind is the seat of discernment, and the belly is the seat of action. Each center is important to our sense of well-being. No less important is the relationship and interaction among the three centers. Look for the three centers to work together. Trust and respect the workings of the three centers as the way to a full life. But if the belly is not happy . . .

The Soft Belly

"One of the major results of Contrology is gaining the mastery of the mind over the complete control of your body."

*– Joseph Pilates, Physical Trainer
and Inventor of Exercise Equipment*

Joseph Pilates combined the influence of gymnastics from his father and the discipline of nursing from his mother, to heal himself. Joseph was a sickly child. He didn't want to gloss over one of his ill conditions without addressing the whole. Being mindful about the body's movement shifted calisthenics to an artform.

Joseph Pilates created an exercise method he referred to as the "Art of Contrology." He developed his method to strengthen his entire body and stimulate a sense of well-being. The key to success in his exercise is to breathe with each movement. The core of which he speaks is the area below the rib cage down to the top of the pelvis bone, from the front to the back.

Strength comes with focusing on movement sparked with the engagement of the belly. Engage by drawing the belly button to the spine. From this engaged belly, reach the arms or legs out to feel a full body stretch. At the heart of Pilates movement is the mental attention to the details of creating a strong belly.

Coordinating the breath with movement is a challenging aspect of practicing Pilates. When asked to focus on something as simple as the breath, the mind becomes rattled. It is normal to get stuck on trying to figure how one could ever breathe in the first place. Most bodies tend to breathe backwards. To breathe backwards is when the body pulls in on the inhale and pushes out during the exhale. Instead of that, do this: Be a balloon, expand the body when air enters. The same balloon deflates when air gushes out. Let the lungs expand during the inhale and contract the lungs during the exhale. Get big with the breath, get small to push the breath out. The tricks the mind and body play with the "in" of the inhale and "ex" of exhale shows we are creatures of habit. Draw breath in – expand; let the breath out – exert movement by first contracting the core. A person learns the Pilates breath for life.

All forms of exercise improve when awareness is combined with sensation. How the arms and legs move is as important as knowing how the heart and belly move. And it is a good thing the body appreciates the work of each part, invisible or not. The coordination between the breath and body is as important as the body's ability to relax. A body in motion stays in motion. The body at rest stays at rest. An engaged body implies physical tension. Tension thwarts relaxation, obstructs the natural flow, and stifles the instincts.

The opening of the treasure chest of my heart led me to the giant in my mind. The awakened giant of my mind, guided me to sink into my belly. Taking time to let my attention fall into my belly revealed the feeling of a heavy, dense object. My belly began to communicate with me. In my belly, I experienced what felt like a lump of clay.

Digesting Life

"Contemplation is to knowledge what digestion is to food –
the way to get life out of it."

– Tryon Edwards, Theologian

The belly intelligently acquires and applies skills and knowledge. At a very basic level, hunger is a message from the belly. Yet, the body also can signal hunger when thirsty. The belly does not function well when tense or neglected and is sensitive to internal and external turmoil. The belly offers immediate feedback about the digestibility of each decision. When a decision is digestible, all is well. When a decision disagrees with the system there is a sense of upset. Learn to discern the importance of an internal response sparked by an external stimulus. Practice the art of knowing when things are not right as early as possible. A limited world view grows like a cancer while daydreaming. Ignoring belly messages, will prompt other warnings.

Discomfort increases as awareness of what the body needs to nourish itself decreases. The more thought about what the body needs tends to dull the senses in deciding what best to eat. The operative word is THINK. Stop thinking and let the intelligence of the belly come through. Let the belly do its job.

The belly's job once forgotten is then ignored. My attention to the belly was distracted by the loud calls of the heart and the mind. My heart center called for attention from the ignorance of hiding what I did not want to see nor feel. When I started to hear the muffled cries for the return to innocence, my heart craved to be free from the dark entertainment of turmoil. My mind was serving a life-long prison sentence of ruminating over the same thought forms in the same order. The mind had forgotten how to be free from the pressure of dictates and dictators. A momentary pause was enough of a gap to disrupt old antiquated habits that no longer fit into what was currently needed for me to exist. This push to stay the same and the pull into a new world distracted my attention from what was, to what could be. I wrestled with what could be important to me. I learned that I, not my perceived limitations could manage life better. I could, not anyone else, rid myself of those things that I had accepted as out of my control.

I had replaced heartfelt love and peace of mind with worry and frustration. I was no longer a creator of love, rather a victim of a habit fabricated to serve others. There was a sick pride in the amount of craziness I could handle while fixated to welcome more. The overflow of craziness dumps raw garbage into an unsuspecting belly. Dense and heavy. Fast and hard. There is never enough time to prepare a defense for the unsuspecting belly.

Lump of Clay

"A vessel is formed from a lump of clay with care, however, it is the empty space within the vessel that makes it useful."

– Tao Tzu, Philosopher and Writer

This massive, undigested garbage laid heavy in my belly and revealed itself as a lump of clay. Clay is the marriage of the elements of earth and water. The moist environment of the belly kept the clay soft, pliable, and moldable. This lump of clay was ready and waiting to take a form. The clay cared not if the form was that of a cup, a bowl, a vase, a pitcher, a tube, or a brick. The lump was ready to claim its purpose, be it to serve or hold space. This lump of clay did not have dried edges, didn't appear hard, or resistant to form something. This lump of clay was alive, vibrant, red, and earthy. This lump of clay, peaked the curiosity of my heart and mind. My heart's innocent love created space to honor the unfolding of the reveal. My mind discerned the need for time and respected this symbolic lump of clay.

A human's nature is either reserved or ready to jump into action. Jumping into action skips over the possibility that there is nothing that needs to be done. The lump of clay was fine being a lump of clay. There was no rush to come into form. The richness and the beauty of the lump of clay was the mere possibility of being creative. My gift of clay signaled that my purpose was not always a final product, but for me to stay in the realm of possibility. I needed to do nothing more than live in the realization of I am a creative creature.

The Way of the Belly

"The belly is the commanding part of the body."

– *Homer, Poet and Author*

Imagine a belly constipated with unresolved issues. A belly consumed by endless servings of tension and fear offers little value to the whole. Churning about the same old thought preoccupies the belly when the belly is capable of much more.

There are two parts to the digestion system, the mechanical and the chemical. The mechanical piece includes the mouth, teeth, throat, esophagus, and intestines. The chemical side is the fluids produced because of the sight, smell, and introduction of food to the system. The thought of food can get the mouth salivating and the stomach to begin contracting. This is the body preparing to receive food by alerting the muscles to get ready. The food placed in the mouth moves the salivary glands to flow more. The intestines begin to leak chemicals in preparation to receive food. From the mouth, pushed down the throat, to the belly, the body breaks down food to bits and then to mush. The small intestine's wave-like contractions release the food's nutrients. The nutrients absorb into the body as energy or to build and repair muscle, tissue, bone. What remains is the fiber that is pushed out of the system.

That is the way the belly digests food. How does the belly work with thoughts and emotions? When preparing to meet with the belly, calm the rest of the body, the heart, and the mind. The best time to dialogue with the belly is after digestion, or before hunger signals. Nudge the belly with a question about whether there is a sense of satisfaction or melancholy.

Is the digestive system willing to work with thoughts, feelings and emotions? Digesting thoughts is still a two-part system. There is the physical response and an energetic aspect to digesting the fruits of thinking. The breath and heart patterns change. The body may become juicy or dehydrated. The vision turns inward or becomes blurred by tears. Smell the burning brain cells that fume and vacillate between facts and fiction. The body is on high alert and prepares to attack or retreat. The thoughts parked in the mind start the imagination flowing. The belly begins to leak chemicals in preparation to receive the emotions. The feelings, not expressed through the mouth, are pushed down the throat, to the belly. The body breaks down the feelings to bits and then to mush. Spasms pass through each cell as it experiences the feeling of joy or pain. Once the thought, feeling or emotion is digested, there is choice in what comes next. The choice is as simple as labeling the remains of the thought as a building block or an anchor and then filed for future reference.

The view of this internal working of the belly complements one's view of the world, as a process or a miracle. Both process and miracle come through as attitude and the words chosen to explain how the world works. To keep things moving, keep filling the belly with cardboard or nutrition.

Our choice in sustenance reflects a subtle personal philosophy. Is there a willingness to try something new or satisfied with the comfort of the way things are? When life is exciting, is it a sense of satisfaction or hunger for more? Is there comfort in being alone or is the feeling a craving for attention? The well-being of the belly reflects the quality of life. Now that is something to chew on.

How to Act

"How we think shows through in how we act.
Attitudes are mirrors of the mind.
They reflect thinking."

– David Joseph Schwartz,
Motivational Writer and Coach

Life is a dance where the heart, mind, and belly partner in rhythm with love, discernment, and action. The dance is choreographed first in the safety of the darkness, then shared in the presence of community, families, and friends. The private dance is part of the advancement of the individual and contributes to the spirit of the collective whole. The way the world responds to the dance, suggests the value of the contribution. The more people behave in a way that is acceptable to others, the greater the likelihood of living in an adaptable culture. Without the dance, without adaptation, the gap between people silently widens in a society of respectful indifference and tamed courage.

The relationship between the individual and the world is mutual. The individual contributes to the collective and the collective shapes the development of the individual. As the individual is greater than the sum of its three centers, the planet earth is greater than the presence of its inhabitants. The individual has a heart, mind, and belly and the planet has a heart, mind, and belly. The energy of the planet interacts with her inhabitants. With heart, the earth gives and receives. The planetary mind gathers and retains information and follows form. The planetary belly accepts, grinds, discards. The planet adjusts with each withdrawal and deposit.

No one knows the full capability of what the earth can withstand and for how long. If there isn't, there should be a growing concern about how human action impacts the future of the planet. How much is too much before the natural order and balance tips out of control? A conservative approach is to weigh short-term benefits against long-term welfare. How about not testing the earth's limits, but to humble ourselves as humans and proceed with modesty. It is best to ask permission first, rather than risk irreparable damage while begging for forgiveness. Second chances are not guaranteed.

Humans need to believe the world is here for us. What needs to be understood is that the earth will continue to exist without humans. The individual consequences of violating personal guidelines may have little impact. When consequences appear greater than a quick solution, rules are created to control the multitudes. The power of a rule is true for the individual when it is also true for the masses. When the results are the same for everyone and following the rule benefits all, it is a good law.

For instance, the act of a single piece of trash thrown on the ground is manageable. When everyone feels free to dump their trash on the side of the road, there is a problem. The consequences of litter tarnish the beauty of the landscape with piles of trash and tickle the underbelly of a health issue. A law can be created to punish people who litter, but will the problem be solved? Is the problem simply littering or living in a society where littering is acceptable? Littering is a modest example.

The land is being stripped of its natural resources and the waters are being poisoned. There is a lack of constraint on pollutants and the impact on the welfare of future generations is unknown. Laws created to place restrictions on an action miss the mark of being effective. Actions that come from a need are less likely to be resolved by a law. A litter law, for example, may be well written, but if the need to litter remains greater than the consequences of breaking the law, the law will fail. It is the need to litter, not the effectiveness of a law, that requires investigation.

A person believes that the world would be a better place if everyone else just thought the same way they did. That is a fancy dream. People do not feel the same way, do not think the same things, and do not act the same way, for the same reasons. People are accustomed to get along or not. Beyond rules and laws, a society operates within a set of unspoken agreements, based on an implied understanding.

A driver's license requires a written and practical exam to prove the capability of operating a motor vehicle. A license is about all the proof needed. Periodically the license needs to be renewed to prove we are still alive. When ready to sit behind the wheel of a car, there is no need to arrange a meeting with all the other drivers in the vicinity. Trust infers that everyone knows which side of the street to drive. By sitting behind the wheel of a car with a license, an unspoken agreement is entered with all the other drivers on the road that everyone knows what they are doing.

Social engagements fall in the realm of unspoken agreements. For example, dating is about two people finding out how one's idea of courting compares with the other's idea. As the relationship grows, the agreement is modified to include what is acceptable, what is not, how to play fair, and how to get along as a happy couple. Marriage is the agreement to officially transfer courting into a legal union. The ceremony to sign the marriage certificate eclipses the original unspoken agreement. The marriage vows assume nothing changes from the unspoken agreement and adds a layer of responsibility as two individuals become husband and wife.

Common courtesy is a form of unspoken agreements. A culture melds common courtesy and unspoken agreements, move from one way of being into another as the nuances of life occur. Shades of difference in shifts of political power and socio-economic fluctuations can erase and redraw lines around the definition of common courtesy. Common courtesy, as well as common sense, is not so common.

Regarding rules, laws, unspoken agreements, and common sense, how are we supposed to act? The Golden Rule as adopted by Christians is, "Do unto others as you would have them do unto you." Judaism offers a version of the same rule as, "What is hateful to you, do not to your fellowman. That is the entire Law, all the rest is commentary." Islam proposes, "None of you is a believer until he desires for his brother what he desires for himself." The Native American affirms, "In the beginning were the instructions. They are to love and respect all living creatures and Mother Earth."

The Golden Rule reflects a concept of what it means to be kind and gentle in this world. There are instances when doing unto others as you would have them undo to you sometimes fall short. Consider, for example, that a rule can be considered golden when appropriate action is something done or desired simply because it is the right thing to do. It has no bearing on how other people would consider – or appreciate – it. The test is for an action to be good and beneficial, true to the self and for all people. Anything other than that suggests a critical nature. The way we show up in this world is the test of how the belly responds.

Belly Blocks

"Trust your hunches. They're usually based on facts filed away just below the conscious level."

– Dr. Joyce Brothers, Psychologist and Columnist

No one knows what is going to happen next. When something happens, it is not immediately known if the action is good or bad. If the belief is that life is good, then all that happens as it is either way, can be accepted good or bad. If the perception that an action is good, then all is well. If the perception that an action is bad, wait to see what comes next. Since life is good, the story is not over until the outcome is good. The only thing that never changes is that everything changes. The fear of the unknown blocks the next steps in life. Results are not predictable. Attempting to predict the future obstructs the view from the heart, mind, and belly. Trust.

Procrastination is a close cousin to blockage. Opportunities diminish when there is a refusal to act. Time passes while mulling over, crawling through, and meandering around the limitless puddle of "what ifs," while waiting for a sign. Bottomless rabbit holes of possibility hide behind hidden stumbling blocks. We know only what we know. We can know what we don't know, but we have no idea of what we don't know we don't know. Although we have no control over what happens, we can control our attitude. Trust.

We do have control of what we put into the belly. Overindulgence is easy. Holidays invite the opportunity to overeat, over drink, and overstay our welcome. That is not the case for us, it must be somebody else. As a society, attribute it to consumerism or human nature, people create excuses to celebrate. Some days are created for the single reason to celebrate overindulging. The Friday after Thanksgiving, St. Patrick's Day, and Cinco de Mayo are examples. Celebrating a "holiday" is only one excuse to relinquish control. Common sense bows to consumption when the moment arises, or the desire to be a part of something bigger. We consume too much, of too many things, too soon, too quickly. We know when something isn't good for us and do so anyway for the sake of a good time. Trust.

The same way food and drink are consumed into the belly, thoughts and emotions feed actions as well. Diet consists of the combined influences of all the senses: what we watch, what we hear, what we taste, what we touch, and what we smell. Also, include what we "sense" intuitively. Our surroundings impact decisions and how to show up. People around us impact our thoughts, decisions, and what is said. When outside influence is greater than an inward sense of constraint, prepare to spiral out of control. Trust.

Why Now

"Now is the time. Now is the time to know that all that you do is sacred."

– Hafez, Persian Poet

I lived for decades without appreciating the worth of my heart. Five years passed until I learned about the magnitude of my mind. My life became rich with possibility. I experienced life with an open heart, connected to the opening of my mind. My learning curve flattened. Within five months I came into my belly. I now sit to assemble the pieces of life wondering what the image of this puzzle will reveal about me, to me. What is it from my life that I am to know now?

Before stepping into life from this day forward, pause with appreciation. Each group of people comes with a creation story telling the world how the ancestors came to be. Creation stories include examples and guidelines of how to treat each other. Buddhists have Four Nobel Truths and the Eight-Fold Path, and the Old Testament offers the Ten Commandments. By knowing the past, there is an idea about the future.

I was born and raised during the 1950s. My father wanted to own land and build his home with his own hands. My father was the epitome of a self-made man. The fifties introduced modern conveniences resulting in less chores and more leisure time. There are types of people who are the first to adopt and buy into anything new. Then there was my father. He was a recycler before recycling was a thing. He was the champion of repurposing because he threw nothing away. He personified the zero-carbon footprint. He accepted full responsibility for himself. When he was a youngster, he spent the Great Depression as a son of a mother who worked to keep things together. His experience of the Depression was that his mother struggled; her struggle was his world view. As an adult, he claimed his success was due to his own hard work. He allowed little room for distraction. He separated his work life from his family life. He had his job and he provided for his wife and children. He made sure to take care of his responsibilities and knew he was better off than the guys with whom he worked. He saw the difference in people and held firm to his beliefs and opinions about them. As he aged he became a collector of all sorts of gizmos and gadgets. He held his possessions as he held his beliefs. He let the dust cover them, never looking at them to question whether they remained relevant or useful.

The days of modern convenience expanded the world beyond the fence and encouraged independent living. The whole wide world came into the living room through a tiny, black and white television. I learned what was going on in the world during the evening news. I can't remember, so I guess news stories have always contained a hint of sensationalism. The one journalism class I took in college taught me that news reporters stay clear of their opinion and stick with the facts. What has changed is that the object of the message has become subjective. The more entertaining the story, the more newspapers sold, and more viewers tuned in. Despite the human tolls of war, conflicts between nations remain. Conflict is what makes news. The profits of war boost the economy and those willing to invest in war, become wealthy. The words describing conflict are charged with emotion and struggle for power, ownership, control, and resources. Has the nature of conflict ever been understood?

Conflicts of the 1960's were over opinions about the value of war and violation of human rights. Families struggled to coexist in a world, aware of the evils of nuclear war. Lines of power were drawn as politicians negotiated the cold war. Those lines shifted as peacemakers attempted to control the use of nuclear weapons. I remember being seven years old and curled up in the armchair of the living room watching the United States and Russia figure out the Cuban crisis on television. I remember huddling on the cold tile floor of the hallways in my elementary school. Small children, crammed into an even smaller, dark, book repository as the teacher read books to occupy our young minds while minutes ticked away until the all clear bell signaled time to return to the classroom. School, the place children and teachers learned and practiced how to survive a nuclear blast.

The physical conflicts weren't kept outside the country. The human rights of citizens within the United States were being violated, all because of the color of skin. I was witness to the leaders being assassinated. The President John F Kennedy. His brother, Attorney General and presidential candidate Robert Kennedy. Martin Luther King Jr., a civil-rights leader, socialist, and pastor. All were laid to rest as the struggle for power continued. Struggles came in the form of riots, social reform, and political movements. The effort to protect civil rights, tested the country's resolve and determination. Society and the American ideals were imploding.

The adults of the 1960s became the elders as their parents, the members of the Lost Generation, began to die in the '80s and '90s. As night follows day, the Silent Generation began to die. Their children, the Baby Boomers, now fill the space as the elders for their children. Could the unrest of the '60s have been the beginning of the movement to know thyself? Making sense of internal processes seemed easier than figuring out what was going on in the world. The outward expression of conflict may have sparked the internal nudge for change. The cry was loud, but not everyone heard the call and not all who heard, responded.

It is hard to know whether life is better now for today's children than it was a half century ago. People adjusted to accommodate that sense of unrelenting doom and destruction, and that sense of doom overshadows the news and still feeds on innocence. This filter of doom cannot help but affect decisions for today's actions which influence what happens tomorrow. If today's actions are responsible for tomorrow, then it is time to reconsider a few things.

Passing of Elders

"We are all visitors to this time, this place. We are just passing through. Our purpose here is to observe, to learn, to grow, to love . . . and then we return home."

– An Australian Aboriginal Proverb

Some of life's more important aspects come through when observing the process of the death of the elders. My father died at home, as he had wanted. A year after his death, I sat with my dying aunt. I learned about life and death through her reflections and words. The opportunity for growth is available at any age. When permitted, beauty and appreciation of freedom can come from experiencing another human's death. I assumed responsibility to hold space while another made their transition. My 99-year-old aunt told me that no one knows what old is until they are there. There is no way to share the personal transition of what happens when old age appears. My aunt was amazed at what old felt like. She reiterated that there is no way to prepare the self or another when that time comes. The best anyone can do is to be at peace in the here and now.

My aunt was vibrant, full of life, and responsible for her well-being until the time of her accident. She was clear that she did not fall. It was because of another woman's chair leg that stuck out too far in her path that caused her to trip. Nonetheless, the accident resulted in a broken hip. The break required surgery, if she held the thought of ever walking again. Without surgery, she would be unable to walk. If she remained bedridden, the doctor said, she would live from six months to a year. My aunt decided to have the surgery, yet, she never walked on her own again. Even with the surgery, she died right at six months.

As painful as it was for her, the last week of her life was a gift to me. I am blessed by the experience of being by her side during those minutes, hours, days, and nights. During that week, she and I discussed the possibility of life after death. She talked about her preference of burial or cremation. She pondered why she was still alive. She lived seven days past the day I received the call to come quickly if I wanted to see her one last time before she died. My racing to her bedside that day wasn't for me. My aunt was clear that she did not want to die alone. She had been there for her mother's passing and expected the same for herself.

Those seven days happened during the week between Christmas and New Year's. This was a time of celebration for most, but it was the solemn final days for my aunt. The fifth evening of her transition was the most eventful. I had never seen her in such a heightened state of irritation from trying to make sense of the noise in her head. She told me to talk to her. I spoke of things I knew nothing of, but it made sense to her. She calmed down until my words didn't calm her any more. She told me to be quiet. The energy escalated about her bed. I felt it necessary to move away from her bedside to a wing-backed chair in the corner of her room.

There was a growing intensity within the room. She wrestled with her own demons. She communicated with a congregation of invisible entities that came to be with her. Be they angels, ancestors or spirits, they offered comfort and solace. These entities were now her family and support system. I watched and listened as she spoke to her review board of counselors and judges. The energy in the room grew again as I attempted to become part of the wall. The illumination of the single lamp paled when the room filled with an intense vibration. The iridescent light popped into a bright yellow gold radiance. I don't know how long I sat there until the room returned to its familiar glow. The light of the room changed three times that night as the energy of the room remained at a constant high vibration.

My aunt shifted between her heart and her mind. Her belly had been silent since her fall. She shifted from being uncomfortable to experiencing a mental fire storm. She surfed waves of emotional upheaval. She spoke in unrecognizable languages. She yelled, whispered, and pleaded. She fought until she made peace with this world. Out on that edge, her spirit surrendered. She was ready. Now was the time for her body to follow. But that would not happen for one more evening and two more sunrises.

My aunt was at peace with having been totally responsible for the success in her life. During that evening, I sat in honor and respect of my aunt. She had built a life for herself, independent from all others. She had loved, and she had lost. She knew who she was, and she knew what she wanted. I wondered if now, when her life appeared limited, was she satisfied with her life as full and complete.

After my father died, my aunt saw the opportunity to slip into the empty spot he left behind. She could then fill his place and rely upon my mother's attention. When her brother, my father, died, she expected that my mother would have more time for her. That was not the case. My mother's own depression and grief were all-consuming. Both women were afraid and suffering. Both had needs greater than any one human could hold. And there was no way to soften the pain or fill the void left by the loss of their vitality.

That night of my aunt's reconciliation was a turning point. The energy shifted as if the angels were trying to lift her, yet she remained grounded to this earth. It was as if she needed something and didn't know what it was. She had spent a lifetime fighting for herself, for what she wanted, and what she thought she deserved. Her habit of putting herself first no longer served her purpose. Now her purpose was to die.

That week between Christmas and New Year's was the second time in the past six months she was ready to die. The first time was during the recovery from her hip operation. She believed she was dying, but it was only the after effect of the anesthesia. In the intensive care unit bed, she assumed the staff was doing more than necessary to keep her alive. She had been adamant about no resuscitation. With a tube down her throat, she communicated with me through her eyes. She asked, rather demanded to know, how was this tube down her throat not resuscitation. All efforts to aid her recovery were immediately suspended, as the staff honored her wishes. There she lay in the intensive-care hospital bed unsupported, left alone. Her family and the hospital staff honored her belief that she was dying.

She told me goodbye as she relaxed her body deep into the bed and closed her eyes. To her dismay, forty-five minutes later she awoke from her nap. She was still in the same room with me rather than in the arms of St. Peter. A couple of days later, she transferred to hospice, but still didn't die. Her strength and determination kept her alive. After ten days in hospice, she returned to her assisted living home. There she remained until the final day of her life.

I shifted through my recollections of the past six months as I sat witness that sacred fifth night, as the night of her reunion continued. Waves of light energy filled and emptied the room. The cleansing of her soul, the release of all the secrets she held during her life, came to pass. What had appeared to be one thing resolved into another. There was a moment of peace and then she declared her own death and demanded God take her now. Her petition was clear, "Let my body die." There was nothing more she wanted. Death was close, but this moment was not her time to leave. She lay on her death bed, exhausted, covered in sweat, but never a tear from her eye. She continued to beg God to hear her prayer. She had made her peace, received her penance, and now waited. My prayer was "Let her wait be quiet." And quiet it was.

So It Was

"Just walk beside me and by my friend."

– Albert Camus, Author and Journalist

The morning of New Year's Eve, I stood at the bathroom sink in my aunt's care center. I looked at myself. I searched my eyes. I wondered who was looking back at me. I yearned for the comfort of my bed and the arms of my companion. I wanted to be in my home. When I returned to her bedside, I leaned over her small, still body. Not knowing whether she would hear me, I whispered in her ear that at the end of the day I would go home. For the first time in more than a week I wanted to sleep in my bed. I promised her I would return the next morning. And there I stood.

The night-time caretaker came in to say Happy New Year and good-bye as her shift was over. She told my sleeping aunt she would return in a couple of days. The caretaker and I talked about the power of reciting the Rosary. As she and I talked about life happening in God's time, my aunt exhaled her final breath. I had imagined the sound of the breath leaving the body. The sound of my aunt's last breath was more of a gasp. This moment was one more time for her to bring in that precious life force. To hold on to it one more time before it escaped her open mouth. She could have opened her eyes to see and her mouth to speak and did not. This gasp was her final act. Her spirit had left two days before, hovering over a body that had already taken its final bow. And now, all was at rest.

Being witness to the birth of my grandchildren and awake for the birth of my own children, I know how messy birth is. I was aware of the physical pressure of pushing a human body through the birth canal. I experienced the out-of-body feeling of release by all my physical functions. I let the wisdom of my body take over and handle with care the business of delivering a human being. I felt the presence of the staff act as my support system in the room, coach me to breathe as they held their own breath. I felt the collective push of all those present in the room to deliver my baby.

Now, I was witness to the process of death. Death is no cleaner than birth. Death is messy. I entered this life innocent. I strive to exit with the hope of some semblance of the same innocence. I arrived with nothing. I will leave behind only a collection of memories and influences.

Be that what it may, I can say that I did it. I live it. I leave it. And I aim to do so with sweet resolve. I am here – no longer a child and not quite done.

THE BALANCING POINT

"The best and safest thing is to keep a balance in your life, acknowledge the great powers around us and in us. If you can do that, and live that way, you are really a wise man."

– Euripides, Tragedy Playwright

P ower, conquest, loss, passion, healing are elements for a good self-discovery story. Stories are created and shared to teach others the importance of balance and wholeness. The tales of King Arthur is such a story. From the sword in the stone, to the knights of the Round Table, and the quest for the Holy Grail. Books and movies share the story with various interpretations regarding the symbolic significance of King Arthur. Once the mind navigates levels of understanding, the heart gladly follows. Critics relish a multi-dimensional plot dissecting it into its pieces, true or not. The gift is the ability to use what is received from the story toward self-discovery.

Merlin the Magician taught Arthur the spiritual importance of being king. King Arthur's battles begin with an internal struggle with ego. The Excalibur was his sword of truth. Arthur's false ego was the stone which held the sword until released, not by his strength, but by his innocence. Arthur broke his double-edged sword in two pieces when he abused his power to defend his false ego. Arthur repented and promised to use his power for good. His sword, his birthright, was returned in one piece by the Lady of the

Lake. The Lady represents the Holy Spirit and the lake represents the fluidity of consciousness. From this higher level of good, Arthur ruled his kingdom from his Round Table, a table where there was no one seat with greater relevance than any other. The challenges and battles discussed around the table were about how to maintain or improve the greater good. As the lake represented consciousness, Arthur sought a greater consciousness. Not until Arthur began to seek a greater consciousness, did it become unavailable and lost. Arthur sent his knights into the world to find the vessel of the higher consciousness, the Holy Grail. Darkness and defeat came over the kingdom until the light returned with the knowledge that the Holy Grail is within each of us.

To heal is the return to being whole. Being whole is honoring the power and the inclusion of all that is our birthright. The heart, mind, and belly represent the totality of who we are. When whole, complete and free, we are in ownership of our power. And when power is ignored, the choice is to stay right there or move along.

People are good. We lose sight of our goodness as we forget how to be genuine and authentic. There is a time to stop asking questions and begin to trust. Speak with confidence from a solid core of the heart, mind, and belly. What does a strong, genuine, authentic core look like? Seek not outside, rather recognize it from within. Save time by having an idea of what a personal sense of good means, before seeking and owning it. Know what good looks like in the world, to recognize it in our life and the lives of others. Carry a living dialogue with the nature of good as if it is a gift that keeps giving, keeps growing. Living a life striving toward a greater good is an honorable purpose.

Holding a greater good in mind as a fixed goal is like following a compass pointed to an unwavering truth. Depositing such an ideal close to the heart, is the motivation to climb the peaks and traverse the valleys of life. That spark of wonder keeps us moving, through the hallways of elementary school, to the playing fields of high school, and into college classrooms. It is our interests that pave the path for a career, a path traveled into retirement. We fan our spark to strive, provide, set goals, and do what needs to happen to make it through another day. This 24-hour cycle of sunrise and sunset makes no sense without a grand purpose.

Parents

"Parents can only give good advice, but the final forming of a person's character lies in their own hands."

– Anne Frank, Diarist

People learn how to relate with others based on their first relationship – parents. We gain the knowledge of what it means to be in relation with another, what works and doesn't work. Eventually, experience reveals a sense of what it takes to be a parent. As a parent, when concentrating only on raising a child to be a good adult, the effort falls short. Of course, there is care for the well-being of the children. The heart, mind, and belly awaken to be the best they can be. And yet, when parent's total existence revolves about that child, their contribution lacks pizzazz. The problem with having a world view only as a parent, is that when the children leave home, the parent is left alone and lost. Consider the person who invests their entire sense of self as a parent. Without developing themselves as a full person, they only age – but do not mature. The other extreme is the parent who takes raising their children for granted. Their limited view is that the child will always be there. If the child will always be there, then this parent has excused themselves from the child's life. Attending a child's concert is optional because there will always be another. No need to go to the ball game because there will always be another ball game. Then the day comes for the child to cross the graduation stage to the parent's cries of pain over all the lost time.

The parents of adult children hope their ability as parents has been adequate. Still time is spent wondering whether the effort was enough, fair enough, loving enough. Was enough given to keep the cycle of goodness moving forward? This idea of being a nurturing source for a child's growth is true beyond playing the role of parent. Expand the idea of raising a child to how any other relationship is given birth. All relationships share the investment of time and effort for the future of those who remain behind when the end of time comes.

Those who chose not to be a parent remain a child within the Parent-Child relationship. There is reason to respect this dynamic. We are each a link in the chain of life. A parent keeps a mindful eye on the younger ones. The younger ones keep a pulse on all that is happening.

Besides, what is the use of anything if the thing is not applied to heal, inspire, or uplift? The idea of purpose lacks meaning if not accompanied by an opportunity for growth. Imagine a stagnant life. The purpose of life is greater than the acquisition of wealth and property. All this is nothing if it does not raise the bar for at least one other person. Otherwise, we thrash about without direction when actions lack at least a hint of a purpose for the betterment of all.

Love has consequences, thoughts create chain reactions, and actions have after-effects. Love, thought, and actions align with values and morals. Who is responsible for holding those things as true for the elders and imparting that for those younger. Each of us has the potential of being a model. When values and morals benefit only a few, actions become transgressions against humanity. It is not enough to acknowledge that a need exists. A failing system demands attention. It is imperative to push toward an actionable solution.

When stymied as to knowing what to do, pray. Prayer is a suitable action until the right action comes along. Don't stop acting because the perceived solution is incomplete. Act and continue to act until the issue is resolved. Disasters receive loads of attention, yet the efforts to manage the effects of the disaster sometimes fail to make a difference in the lives of those most in need. Help one person and continue to address the needs one at a time until the needs on all levels are met. Actions are how we show up in the world, the gift of what is contained within.

Heal Thyself

"Physician, heal thyself. Teacher, teach yourself."

– St. John of Kronstadt, Archpriest

Training for life is an ever-evolving lesson on self-care. Recognize what taking care of the self is by seeing what it looks like in others. Don't stop there and ignore the necessity of doing so for the self. Notice when fragments of good float by and missed opportunities fade. If they pass again, grab on to these bits of good in such a way that adds to self-care. This is a contribution to a tiny piece of property in the world. Each person has their own set of healing tools, like the ways to calm the mind. Use the tools in an enlightened way that always nurtures the heart, mind, and belly. Maintain a way that is free from the weight and pressure of the unknown.

Healing clears space for being safe in the presence of the unknown. Be comfortable until the nature of confusion breaks down into workable parts. Weigh the parts of confusion as whether they are significant and relevant. Discard the false parts that are heavy and useless to lighten and lift the remaining parts as an offering to release what no longer serves. Image the crap being held within, then release it with an intent to heal the world's needs. Be thankful for the lesson, but let the story go. Wrap the story in love and bury it for good. The natural way of living is as easy as inhaling and exhaling. The natural flow of life and death is being here now.

Healing is to stand on the threshold of beauty. Beauty is the sequence of light, form, and color that pleases the inner and outer eye. In beauty, be willing to struggle with confusion, distraction, and negativity. Let the struggle happen, and then move on because at the other side of confusion is opportunity. In beauty, heal relations with right solutions and valid answers to questions yet to be asked. Feel the fear and hesitation and act anyway. Feel a wave of freshness awaken the stale thoughts and lifeless feelings to rise into being present with courage. Know it as only a habit to perceive a conflict first and recoil into a safe place. Change the habit with love's gentle kiss to explore new ways of being.

The darkest hour is before dawn, but before coming into the light, explore the darkness. The dark nights of the soul are the times to befriend the shades and wrestle with the shadows. When the past is gleaned of its residue and persistence, then all that has been done is enough. Gather what remains to carry on with a happy heart, clear mind, and contented belly. Welcome what needs to be done next.

Simply Be

"Life really is simple but we insist on making it complicated."

– Confucius, Teacher and Philosopher

Be curious. A question initiates the chance to explore the three energy centers. The heart, mind, and belly signals when the time is ripe for portals of possibility to open. Darkness offers a safe environment to delve into the shadows. Accept insight as a credible resource for personal development. The self-discovery process requires drilling down beyond callused layers of cynicism and around shields of doubt. Digging is healing. To dig signifies that the status quo is no longer acceptable. Recognize how resistance shows up to slow the flow until blocked. Attention is the light that breaks down the blockage that interrupts thinking.

Be patient. Engage in a temporary truce to relax attacks and protect the heart while healing. Build a frame of reference to highlight the strength in vulnerability. When each of the centers soften, in its place grows an appreciation of actions as free-flowing and authentic. Wonder what can be uncovered and discovered with opening the treasure chest, waking the sleeping giant, or forming clay. Patience is to hold space as a conduit for good until the goodness is received as a gift.

Be aware. Ask the heart how it is doing, where has it traveled, and, what has it learned. Is the heart satisfied with how love and peace are being expressed? Ask the heart to breathe, expand, to identify and hold the emotion of the moment. Ask the mind to hold an emotion, any emotion. Can the mind hold the emotion longer than a minute or an hour? Can the belly identify what turns it sideways? Spend time to be with the belly and listen for sounds beyond words. Hear the difference as heard from the heart, mind, or belly. Sit with problematic words and play with diverse meanings and interpretations. Sense the birth of an idea that comes from outside the body. A message can come as a feather falling from a bird, or the rustling leaves of a plant when the breeze is silent. The world is here to offer support.

Be calm. Enter the mind with a calm conversation that is different from the noise of a disturbed world. Join a calm mind with an open heart and a happy belly to see what that looks like. Develop a sense for the greatest results of such interplay. Continue to juggle the parts until the magic moves the three centers into synchronicity. Imagine peace and a peaceful approach to life when the mind, heart, and belly conspire together. Return to the mind and expand the concept of thinking by bringing attention to the brow. Feel any pressure, sense any vibration, experience any color. Listen with ears to hear any message from the brow. Harness the experience of jumping all over the place to resting within a calm center. Let the feeling of serenity spread between mind, heart, and belly.

Be courageous. Nothing is ever over. Energy never ceases to exist, it only changes form. When there is a change in form, bring it up in conversation with other people. Find out what is happening with them. Discussing different perspectives about the same experience, develops a new language. The words come first to reflect a shared ideology. Sitting together in the glow of a shared interest stimulates more of the same. Verbalizing words uncovers more things in common than not.

Be bold. Disrupt the ordinary to seek the chance to dip a toe in a river. Notice the different experience of dipping toes in different rivers. A person can never dip their toe in the same river twice. Once the water passes that place on the bank, that river will never be the same again. And chances are that the flow of the water changes the dynamic of the bank. As with the bank or river, the heart, mind, and belly are ever-changing.

Be something. The reason for the journey of seeking and searching for new meaning doesn't need to impact the world in a major way. These moments are a sacred connection with the Divine. This is an invitation to participate in co-creating life. Do this for love, for peace, and happiness. The focus is not on doing but being. Be the love, be the peace – and be there for one another.

No One is Alone

"We are like chameleons, we take our hue and the color of our moral character, from those who are around us."

– John Locke, Philosopher and Physician

Children are born with an innate ability to surrender to the kindness of others. A child is open and willing to receive others as they are. The nature of the innocent is to trust but naivete can offer protection for only so long. Awareness comes about with the realization that consequences accompany expectations and actions. At one end of the spectrum of the emotional state is feeling good when everyone feels good. At the opposite end of the spectrum is pain and suffering. A sidebar at that extreme is perplexity. An environment that was once dependable, pleasurable, and overflowing with loving moments erode into episodes of bewilderment and confusion. A spontaneous life is now sprinkled with hesitation. An outgoing personality withdraws within self-reliance. The safety cloak of invisibility keeps away unsolicited offers wrapped as conditional service. Each layer of protection adds to the feeling of being alone in the world.

Life is a struggle without a reliable set of instructions to rely. The best instructions aren't out in the world or another's library, but internally available as instinctual. The instincts evolve to answer questions that are appropriate for each stage of life. The times of solitude and isolation are the heaviest when compounded with a sense of need. Skepticism taints the goodness others offer with the concern of their demand for something in return. The culture of questioning motive and goodness is self-perpetuating. Hope floats with the remembrance that everyone is doing the best they can with what they know and what they have at that moment.

Everyone enters life a blank slate. Speech is learned by associating words with things. School is the learning ground for putting words together to form sentences. Sentences put together to form paragraphs. Paragraphs form reports and articles. What is not taught is how to read energy and intention that comes with words. There is no training on seeing what lies between the lines. Some are born with a natural appreciation for the subtle, while others wait for their teacher.

While living on this earth, we are members of two families. There is the birth family and the ancestors. The birth family are those who form the family tree. The ancestors of which I refer, include more than the line of descendants, rather the collective wisdom of all those who lived before us. The idea of race, gender, nationality is what this life is about. The collective wisdom includes the knowledge, understanding, and insight of all energetic life forms. Spiritual ancestors hold and care for us. No one is alone. Not before birth, not in this lifetime, nor during the transition from one form to the next. No one is ever alone.

Joni Mitchell sings about being golden stardust, getting back to the place of origin. All elements of this earth originated from the heart of a star. The connection to the universe is greater than an umbilical cord in the womb. After delivery, the umbilical cord connecting the child to their mother is no longer needed. Every child is physically separate from, yet remains emotionally attached to their birth mother. That child cannot separate itself from the universe. The ancestors are forever present and remain silent and hidden until beckoned. Ancestors are not here to interfere, influence, or save us from ourselves in this life. They are here only to support and hold space until all attempts to do so are exhausted. There is no lack of response when the request for help is uttered.

Invisible entities surround us to lighten the heaviness of the heart, mind, and belly. When called upon, they have the wherewithal to release unnecessary, self-imposed bondage. They have the capability to shift thinking, expand the heart, or release the gut. We were intimate with these entities before taking human form. It is by our request to reconnect with the ancestors, who were here long before we arrived on this earth. Think of them often, as one does with a best friend. The term "friend" is a pale comparison to the support of an ancestor.

Ancestors source an unconditional, endless availability of love, support and protection. With confidence, we walk about, knowing their support acts as a safety net. Ancestors are forever traveling partners, rooted in a spiritual support system. Ancestors are ancient and wise beyond human understanding. Everything we know is limited in its understanding and restricted by its definition. The essence of who we are is what ancestors gravitate toward. Earthly life force shares the same essence as the ancestors.

Birth is the moment when everything known about the ancient self is forgotten. The journey through the birth canal prepares the spirit for being in physical form. The birth experience may be more difficult than dying. Entering life strips away any understanding of what is known about the heart, mind, and belly. Death allows us to take what was learned during life with us when we leave.

Humans are simultaneously alike and unique. Each individual has their own set of feelings associated with a set of values and morals. We are familiar with what belongs to us as human and sometimes feelings seem foreign. Those foreign feelings may come from three different causes.

One cause for having unfamiliar feelings may come from another, human – perhaps a family member, a friend or an acquaintance. Their feelings overflow their physical boundaries and pour into unsuspecting receptacles. They look for support. They seek someone else to take over ownership and solve their problems.

The second possible cause is still human, but of the collective-conscience kind. These collections originate from groups, such as a church, clubs, or employers. The group may originate from a place with a little more distance like a favorite grocery store or city council meeting. Or the group may be even as distant as the political workings of the state, nation, hemisphere or the world. Their workings seep through invisible channels into a formidable effect on people.

The third cause of feelings is rooted in and through the ancestors. This ancestor may or may not be a member of the bloodline. The trials of a great-great grandmother left unresolved way back when, pass down and end up in this life. When a problem makes no sense and appears with no cause, it may belong to someone from an earlier time. It came here because the ancestor didn't resolve their problem before passing. Until the feeling is processed, the problem can continue to haunt the next in line.

The phenomenon of inherited feelings that dropped into this life, comes with a choice to either let it continue to the next generation or resolve the issue on behalf of all the ancestors. Being aware of disruptions in life doesn't always feel like it, but it is a gift. The call for help is a request to end the madness. Find the strength to clear the confusion and break the curse. Remember, no one is alone.

A Balanced Life

"Happiness is not a matter of intensity, but of balance, order, rhythm, and harmony."

– Thomas Merton, Priest and Author

When living present in the moment, time is irrelevant. Time is neither fast nor slow, abundant nor scarce. Dance in the present. Glide from one place to the next. Each situation calls on creativity to parse, gather, repeat, delete, or save what is relevant. Forget the doing and instead strive to be important and essential in the moment. Time acts as a measuring device, a direction, a scale, a quantity. Every so often, the internal mechanism needs to be fine-tuned. The tune-up is not according to what is true in this world, but what is true in a greater realm. When standing completely in the moment, there is no leaning into the future nor being pulled by the past. This is being upright and balanced.

A balanced life honors how the heart, mind, and belly interact with each other and the world. The senses of sight and sound consider the interaction as being proper. Choice. Choose to be here and now or choose to explore new ways of being. Choose whether to be sensitive to the nuances of the mind, to either just hear words, or listen carefully to what is being said. Listening rather than hearing, is the way to gather more information for a greater array of options. When the awareness of how many options are available, the pressure of choice is no longer overwhelming. When life comes about from choice, actions and their outcome are different. The outcome is more predictable rather than wrapped around the axis of confusion.

A gap exists between receiving information and action. In that space breathe into the heart and feel the breath travel throughout the body. Draw life into being with intention, like the very next move depends upon it.

Boundaries Not Walls

"Love yourself enough to set boundaries. Your time and energy are precious. You get to choose how you use it. You teach people how to treat you by deciding what you will and won't accept."

– Annie Edson Taylor, Teacher and Adventurer

Regardless of the work to create a strong heart, mind, and belly, the need for protection continues to exist. One form of protection is to declare a boundary. A declared boundary watches out for uncertainty and mitigates risk. When confidence waivers, a temporary boundary serves in the interim. So, first, explore what a personal boundary looks like.

Boundaries takes shape in different ways to guard against people and under various circumstances. Ask the heart a few questions about the purpose of the boundary. If asking a question feels too personal, then ask the question of the situation. Do I live in a war-torn or a third-world country? Ask it. Am I safe in my neighborhood or workplace? Ask it. Each answer, every impulse received, requires consideration as a valid concern. Determine if the boundary is to encompass the entire body, or if not, beyond to the community or the world. The safer we feel, the smaller the boundary. The purpose of the boundary is for self-preservation.

Sensitive people need to consider their feeling of overwhelm. Imagine a layer of protection around only the effected energy bodies. Or, imagine wrapping each of the heart, mind, and belly with their own protective boundary. Visualize a boundary of safety. A benefit of knowing boundaries, is to know when we push up against someone else's boundary. Take a breath and be respectful of the boundaries established by others.

Associate a building material when imaging the boundary. Build the boundary with a substance that provides the level of safety needed for the situation. The protection can be with a stream of light, cloth, glass or titanium. Call boundaries into place when leaving the house and retract them when entering a safe place. Remember to allow the boundaries to relax from time to time.

A boundary may offer protection from an old story until time allows the reframing of it. A boundary is in place for protection until the threat has passed. When hearing of an unfortunate event, the immediate reaction may be to seek cover based on a false fear of an irrelevant situation. Being wrapped as tight as a cocoon, separated, and isolated, imposes a personal concern on others.

The exterior of the boundary happens with an intent. A rough exterior created to scare away evil spirits, mean people, and small children may gain power. If an abrasive exterior can scare away evil spirits, then what's to say that the interior, the heart, mind, or belly, isn't afraid as well.

Keep the boundary dynamic. Invoke it when necessary, yet let it retire when no longer needed.

Peace in Balance

"You cannot find peace by avoiding life."

– Virginia Woolf, Writer and Modernist

Fresh, light, and comfortable happens within the calm as the heart, mind, and belly work together. Calm sets the stage to thrive in an unpredictable, crazy world. Truth comes with a sense of peace as pure and free from the pressure of what others may think as right and appropriate. Such peace is bold and unapologetic. Balance and harmony are characteristics within the realm of good will. All this goodness, when consistent and equitable constructs a place of agreement. Not to be lulled into complacency, add a measure of readiness.

When faced with an upset, decide on an action born from a broad concept of self and expect a reasonable outcome. What more could one ask? What more could one want? With a balanced and harmonious heart, mind, and belly, the gift is succeeding in the unpredictability as a way of life. Shift and change, evolve and grow ... with grace.

Take Good Care

"I have come to believe that caring for myself is not self indulgent. Caring for myself is an act of survival."

– Audre Lorde, Writer and Activist

Come home. Home is the place of the heart, the mind, and the belly. Be as kind and gentle with the self as when called upon to be as caring with any other innocent living being. Amid chaos, the advice of others is usually something they best keep to themselves. These four little words "take care of yourself" offer nothing. The way of taking care of self is contrary to what the world is currently needing.

Take care. Be clear about the resources available in the treasure chest of the heart, measure the health and vitality of the giant of the mind, ensure the flexibility of the clay is present in the belly. Taking care is a balancing act. The outside world that is crying for attention must be balanced with the internal world, which is easier to ignore. Nonetheless, the sense of self withers quickly with a suggestion of neglect. Everything that is of the world, let return to the world. All that is of the essence, hold close as a gift, a treasure, and inheritance.

Forgiveness. Honor the heart, mind, and belly with the inclusion of soft compassion in self-care. Forgiveness of self is the soothing balm for wounds and freedom of the centers to reengage with life. Forgiveness nourishes the sense of peace with a cyclic nature of unwavering mercy.

Forgiveness is the realm of acceptance that a thing is neither right nor wrong, it just is. Peace is cohabiting with the existence of an injustice as forgiven to the extent of accepting it occurred, but never a hope of denial that it ever happened.

Forgiveness and acceptance. In the instances when the wounds are deep, there is no switch to turn forgiveness on or off without time in reflection. The definition of acceptance may require modification and expansion. A violated sense of self needs to understand that forgiveness and acceptance is not a single, simple act, once and done. Forgiveness is a process that requires vigilance and daily renewal. Acceptance is the ability to be called back to face a multi-faceted mental monster with a calm method.

Always something. An event sparks thoughts, feelings and emotions. The details of an event fade, but the effects of the event create momentary chaos. Chaos spins memories that shape reactions and the reactions form habits. When we wake up to being participants in an endless cycle of our own doing, the opportunity to stop reliving the hurt begins. Be willing to sit with the totality of a hurtful moment until the upset dissolves. Stay in quiet reflection to witness the moment lose its charge. Living is a neutral stage of possibility increases time between recall and reaction. This is the moment that allows for the invitation of forgiveness to be sent. The greatest forgiveness is a quality, not a quantity. Aim to regain neutrality one more time to forgive, rather than avoid taking good care.

Joy Over Happiness

"Give happiness and joy to other people. There is nothing greater or better than that."

– Ludwig von Beethoven, Composer

Call joy into the heart, mind, and belly. Happiness is transitory, but joy is an infinite state of being. Happiness is a trickster, but joy can't be silenced or faked. As with sugar, happy tastes good now, elevates the energy, and then there is the letdown. Joy is a light that shines on the path and embraces each opportunity as happy. Joy is an attitude.

Joy is in discovering one's unique style for intuition. The recipe for intuition is youthful curiosity, stout patience, and perceptive vision. Intuition may be as simple as thinking of a friend and then quickly receiving their call. Intuition may be an influence on a course of action, like traveling the same route every day, but one day is different. For some reason a right turn instead of the usual left avoids a traffic jam or leads to the experience of a life-altering adventure. Take a chance to go beyond the comfort zone to see what may happen. This is showing up in life. Let that little shift come from a confidence of knowing joy.

Measure the amount of joy currently filling the heart. The tools of the treasure chest are instruments of joy that create gifts given to the world. Joy is in the breath. Joy is present in the act of loving. Joy adds flavor to the mundane and pops up in unexpected and delightful ways.

Ask the giant in the mind if it is embracing or resisting joy. The story of Goliath in and of itself is a sad tale. He was a victim, indentured soldier, and slave. The giant that blocks thinking feeds on fear and stagnation in unhinged situations. Plant joy in thinking fertilized with possibility. A compromised thought is joyless because it suggests surrender. A new reality born of a fresh perspective, produces possibility for a satisfying middle ground. Think of joy in possibility as its own reward.

Invite joy to penetrate the belly's layers when action stalls. When the will to care for the self is asleep, then act for someone else. Handle conflicting upsets that scream for attention with a joyous act as a gift for the benefit of another. When joy feels sacred, the world is lighter. An act offered in joy is more palatable. The hand is viewed as more likely to help than hurt. If the hand is perceived as harmful and refuted, offer the hand anyway.

The owner of a helping hand is present in the heart, mind, belly. We intuitively know when to extend the hand or when to wait and observe. This comes from being aware of the ebb and flow of balance and harmony. A confident heart supports intuition and decision-making faculties. This is the place to learn how to make a difference in the world one life at a time. Being able to offer a hand in a nonthreatening and acceptable way, is a gift. A helping hand, requires three things.

1. Avoid appearing as an imposition
2. Give without expectation.

3.   Stand in a place of responsibility.

Teachers, nurses, lawyers, and spiritual guides include the practice of offering helping hands. They are either born with or develop the ability to sense confusion in others. They are sensitive to know and honor what is theirs and what comes from others. Honor and respect are important and critical when stepping into another person's life. To make a true difference, make sure that it is for their benefit. It is for their benefit when there is nothing about the gift that is needed. From this place of balance comes joy filled, peaceful actions.

Make It Yours

"The most useful piece of learning for the uses of life is to unlearn what is untrue."

– Antisthenes, Philosopher and Ascetic

This is the platform from which to operate from the heart, mind, and belly. Respect that each center has a certain set of skills. Each center complements the other two. Know that a greater sense of balance is available when the heart, mind, and belly cooperate as a single unit. Have an idea of what the three centers working together looks like and how it may be of benefit to the world.

Reading the final pages of this book suggests the end of a story. There is a sense of accomplishment by turning these last few leaves. Endings can be sweet and sorrowful. Endings don't compare with any other aspect of life. Respect endings with a humble ceremony. The ceremony for finishing a book may be simple. Sip a warm beverage from a decorated ceramic mug. Invite a quiet moment of reflection wrapped in a favorite blanket. Nap under the warm sun. In all cases, let the book soak in.

A book ends with a period. A relationship ends with a slammed door or a sweet goodbye. Life ceases to be physical with the exhalation of animation as the spirit withdraws. Physical death is recognizable. The ending of a relationship is not always as clear because there are false endings, a series of fade outs until the final word. Someone changes their mind or the other apologizes in a way that heals the heart to love another day.

Endings are transitions from one state to another. Some endings, draw out because of a stubborn refusal to submit to the inevitable. Resistance is an opportunity to understand the situation or a single word in a different way. Rather than referring to a thing as ending, try calling it something else, like conclusion. Or perhaps completion, which is another form of wrapping up an issue. The sun sets, the light withdraws. Today is complete. Tomorrow is a new beginning. Awake in the morning dawn as a different person. This is as true as never being able to dip a toe in the same river twice.

Wake up each day with appreciation for the heart, mind, and belly. Declare the day as good. Let the first move be a stepping stone to something great. If the day is a mere continuance of a lackluster yesterday, then let it be a day of reflection. If today is a pause in the cycle of life, then experience it to its fullest. For today is one day closer to entering the portal of the next phase of life.

Our purpose may have been fulfilled during pregnancy. Being the product of the coupling of a man and woman could have been all that was needed. Conception is a powerful act of love or fear. Perhaps a brief existence offers the answer to cure a disease. Or perhaps our purpose was to advance the medical survival of others. The information gathered about the cause of an early death may benefit the future of all children.

Our purpose may rest in the relationship to serve another as they learn through their own struggles. Every day, through every interaction, we change the life of those around us. To do anything less than that suggests this was neither the right time nor the right place, and that is not true. There may be no clear purpose. Life is experienced in many different and diverse ways. Our purpose may rest in a simple walk through life with a sense of purpose.

Growing and learning doesn't stop when being comfortable and present in the heart, mind, and belly. The more we know, the more we grow. A lot of work has already been done. Feel the moment as clear and open. There may no longer be an urgent need to answer the questions of why or how. Knowingly or unknowingly, the first pass through the work, speeds the second opportunity to expand as quickly as possible. Take pause to catch the breath, then carry on.

The energetic movement to expand personal awareness of what it means to be human is in the here and now. Humanity has made leaps and bounds from the time fire was discovered to the exploration of space. With all this knowledge, being human is not the same as when two sticks were rubbed together. There is nothing to stop the capability of the heart, mind, and belly from pushing beyond the space of a new frontier. It is time to push the evolution of humanity because we are better human beings.

Old thought forms nourish new thought fields. Choose whether this moment expands or hinders the experience of life – and accept that it is sometimes both. Regardless of the choice, we are not idle bystanders. As a personal benefit, it is better to be present to make a choice than have the choice made by another. Does it matter if the choice is growth or stagnation? Either way, a lot can happen when life is approached as being new. Each day is a chance to reconnect with the self to begin the day with a new sense of innocence and curiosity. Arrive with a willingness to serve. Our arms are strong enough to uplift another. And do so without expectation.

The time is right. This is a summons to do this now, not because it is important, but because it is relevant and necessary. There is a slice of the population willing and waiting. They are not ready to withdraw, stop exploring, or retire from life. They are motivated to continue to be of service. Their calling is to continue to be a contributor for a better world. They are willing to incorporate their knowledge to lift others. This slice of life knows well that to change the world, they need to start right where they are. They fill the gaps with their understanding. They focus on their corner of the world. They address the issues of those for whom no other help seems appropriate. It is upon that person to know themselves through their own heart, mind, and belly. We are in good company.

And so, it is. Begin to realize where this feeling comes from. The feeling comes from our own interest and curiosity of what is to come next. Life is precious and personal. Life was asking to be of service through a clarified sense of purpose. Although it feels personal and selfish, the desire to be of service is a universal benefit.

Not all people care to answer the call. Fewer still avoid searching for any answer. The answers lay hidden beneath endless possibilities. Questions and answers stimulate the heart to beat, the mind to light up, and the belly to act. What is true? We are responsible for creating our personal truths. What is the purpose of the journey of life? Conception, pass through the birth canal to emerge for the first breath, walk toward the last breath, and finally, be with wisdom. How can any of this be if not for a purpose?

These times are reason enough for standing firm in love, discernment and action. These are turbulent times. The firm ground of standards is beginning to shake. The fear of unfulfilled desires resists living in a complete state of being.

The line between the seen and unseen becomes thinner. What was once clear is now foggy. Discomfort cries for someone or something to come and take away the distress. Quench the desire to fill empty cups of not knowing by opening the door for peace to enter life although there is no sign for push or pull. There is no give and take, there is only give. The hands that used to cling must now remain open to do the work of filling the gap between the haves and the have nots that continues to widen. Aim to neutralize violent acts spoken against humanity that conceals applause and condemnation in the same speech. We are at the point when opinion trumps fact and truth is unimportant. Everyone suffers when profit is more important than people. Let the next new sparkly device invented be free from the cost of another's dignity.

Basic human rights shift from being a right to be a product when there is an opportunity for profit. The definition of basic human rights is being attacked. What is a human right? The right to clean water and fresh air. The right to education. The right of freedom of speech. The freedom to pray or not pray. How about the freedom of life, liberty, and the pursuit of happiness? All of this is being scrutinized. The cry to return to the good old days is futile. There is no going back. There is no fitting in the container of what, because we are much bigger in who we are, how we show up, and what we know.

What now? Take what has been learned and go out to live life in a responsible, caring manner. Model what has been learned for others. Be a mirror for others to reflect upon themselves and the opportunity to come into their own light. Be prepared to accept that there are those not ready for what is being offered. They are place holders. That doesn't mean to force information upon them. Their resistance requires support and guidance through example. Accept the responsibility of being light in their world.

The attempt to be the best remains subjective. We are our own judge, jury, and prosecutor. Respect the need to be fair, honest, and kind, always kind. Create a personal space that includes all the aspects of the heart, mind, and belly. When needed, surround vulnerability with a boundary built to offer temporary protection from the slings and arrows of doubt. Let the boundary shield against the pressure of intrusion. Within that space, gather the strength of love, discernment, and action. Name this space security. Call this sacred space home. When this space is strong enough to stand on its own, withdraw the boundary.

Be open and available to hold another person's hand. As we are not alone, we are not here for ourselves only. We are here for others. We are here as an example. We are here to guide, lift and teach those around us. Prepare to broaden the circle of influence beyond family and beyond friends. As an individual, be here to serve. Together, we light the world.

Settle into a personal understanding of being in the heart, the mind, and the belly. Understanding is the active element that forms the basis of a practice. Nothing else needs to be done other than be. Engaging in the work to build a better world is exhausting. Vitalize this as an exercise, a living practice. Practice is like breathing, necessary and natural. Return the focus on being rather than on doing, but don't do something to avoid doing nothing at all. Add elements from the heart, mind, and belly. If the thought of doing so alone stops progress, then take a small step in any direction until joined by unity with others.

Once a set of reliable tools that support the heart, mind, and belly has been validated, settle into being. The state of being is not a destination. Being is living, breathing, and engaging. Be in touch with the heart, mind, and belly for signs of disruption, desire or desperation. Delve into the nature of desperation as a sign of boredom, exhaustion, or hopelessness. When everything supports love, peace, and agreement, venture into new ways to relate with life.

What was true yesterday, is not necessary or true today. Interactions do not happen in isolation. An interaction sparks one of the three centers and leaves a trace of an effect. All communication, every contact, each interface, all collaboration, every meal, and each night's sleep indeed modify our sense of being. Life's little nuances pass unnoticed when the walk-through happens with vision cast down upon the ground. When experience is limited as being the same old thing day in and day out, the richness of each moment is wasted. Alert the heart, mind, and belly to be ready for each moment in the same vein as one spontaneously creates magic.

Hold those precious moments of being alive in the heart, mind, and belly as sacred. Sacred flashes enhance well-being. When meeting another whole and complete human walking the earth, raise the mark. As the collection of like-minded humans grows through meeting and sharing stories, the conversations elevate us all to a higher level of existence. The experiences within the heart, mind, and belly, help create the collective consciousness. Imagine living in the grace of shared awareness.

This is it. This is one paragraph closer to closing the book and getting on with life. Once the book is closed, wait a moment as an opening of the self occurs. Avoid thinking of the collective or the world. Focus on nurturing the awareness of being present with the heart, mind, and belly. Take a deep breath.

AN EPILOGUE

*"A diamond is a lump of coal that did
well under pressure."*

— *anonymous*

There is one more aside about the three kings of the Old Testament that relates to the heart, mind, and belly. The first king, King Saul, the king of power, represented the power to act. The second king, King David, the king of love, experienced love from its ideal to its destruction. The third king, King Solomon, the king of wisdom, represented the realm of the mind. So, the bible suggests the order of the three centers as belly, heart, and mind.

The arrangement of the books of the bible starts with the story of creation. Adam and Eve were in direct communication with God. Their fall stopped the conversation with the Creator. God then began to speak to His people through His chosen representative. People started doubting that the representative was really communicating with God and revolted against His representative. God started to appoint kings, Saul, David and Solomon, to rule on His behalf. When people revolted against being ruled by the kings, God's word came through prophets. Today, the path seems to be a personal relationship with their source. To do so is the removal of the protective layers covering the heart, mind, and belly.

Human nature is easiest to understand as observed through the innocence of a child. Let us encourage children to be aware of who they are early on and extend opportunity to be a child with childlike playfulness. Love the child unconditionally for they will develop their personal power of how to be a force of good in the world. A child learning responsibility doesn't take away from innocence but contributes to the world being a better place.

From the beginning to the end, there is always one more way to approach life. We just never know because it is not over. Reaching a conclusion is impossible when another leg of the journey is yet to be traveled. May a greater energy than a wing and a prayer move society to a place stronger than its weakest link.

Right action right now seems fluid. I offer this prayer for peace to hold the earth. May an act of respect transform conflict. May the goal of competition be to raise the overall standard of living with no one left behind. May all regard the best investment of profit is building a bright future. Together, let's be honored to raise one another and help them obtain their highest good. And in return, we recognize our reflection in the innocence of every face we meet. Harmony is at its finest when everyone's needs are as important as our own.

"The voyage of discovery is not seeking new landscapes,
but in having new eyes."

– Marcel Proust, Novelist and Critic

ACKNOWLEDGEMENTS

"I cling to my imperfection, as the very essence of my being."

– Anatole France, Poet and Novelist

Everyone has a lesson to teach about life, about ourselves, and about our fears. This book wouldn't be possible without the lessons from the people along my way. The light of day shifted when I awoke to the idea that I live to learn. I am still learning that relationships are reciprocal, and I am very much a part of the equation.

Thank you, teachers. The courageous and spirited ones. The kind and persistent ones. The selfish and selfless ones. Thank you to the ones who called themselves teachers and the ones unaware of their valuable lessons.

Thank you, map makers. To those who allowed me space and kept me safe. To those who supported and encouraged me to go out to the edge and then come back to myself. Thank you for the distinct and hazy reminders that I serve a greater good.

Thank you, gift wrappers. I am who I am today because of charm school and higher education. Thank you to the ones who deemed this important enough for me to attend and saw to it that I did so.

Thank you, fellow travelers, dreamers and sages. To the advisors who helped uncover the hidden gems. To the mentors who were quick to lend a hand or offer a tool. To the savants who smoothed sharp edges and cushioned my falls. To the shamans who shared light to make sense of the ridiculous. To the wizards who cleared the path for publication and beyond.

Please accept my most eternal, heartfelt thank you.

96809691R00107

Made in the USA
Columbia, SC
05 June 2018